# VESTIGES

# OF COURAGE:

## COLLECTED ESSAYS

# VESTIGES

# OF COURAGE:

## COLLECTED ESSAYS

*The Nasiona*

San Francisco

*Vestiges of Courage: Collected Essays*

Copyright © Mireya S. Vela, 2019

Published by *The Nasiona*

For information contact :

nasiona.mail.@gmail.com

https://thenasiona.com/

Cover images by Mireya S. Vela

ISBN: 978-1-950124-03-9

To Dan who helps me love better.

# Contents

# Foreword

*What would happen if one woman told the truth about her life?*
*The world would split open.*
—Muriel Rukeyser

In the beginning they said we were made of mud. A scrap. A hank. A spare bone. Mud is mute and voiceless and so we were supposed to be. We were not the ones who made things happen, so went the story. We were the ones things happened to.

What things? Beatings. Rapes. Being bought and sold. Killings. Shaming. Being ignored. Being erased. Forgotten. And all the casual cruelties of being told we were worthless.

Because we were made of mud and therefore mute, we could not tell the story of these things that kept happening. Isolated in the home, where many such things happened. Kept without education so we could not write our story. Threatened that if we ever were to tell, something much, much worse would happen. Even if we did try to speak, we were not believed. No one knew how to listen to the voice of mud.

For a long time we told ourselves the story that we deserved it, dirty girls that we were. After all, was it not our speech and our hunger to know that forever muddied the perfection of Eden? Had we not sinned, just for being ourselves?

As harsh things kept happening to us, over centuries, we wearied of the old stories. We found ourselves unable to contain all that had happened to us, unable to any longer stifle our being. A fire in the core of our earth bodies cried out for oxygen. And we found a way to make language from the soil of our nature—loam and silt and clay—watered with tears. A language of minerals. A language of algae and fungi. A language of nitrogen. This language grew from our mud of our being and we learned slowly to speak and to hear one another.

As we told and listened to our stories, we came to understand that we *were* making things happen. Life itself. And then its nurturance.

And the world—the ground upon which all of civilization rested—split open.

*** 

As is true of so many of us, terrible things happened to Mireya Vela. In these beautifully and painfully rendered essays, Vela writes about domestic violence as a family norm. She writes about children being abused by male relatives. She writes about rape culture. She writes about the unquestioned assumption that a woman is worth no more than mud, is unentitled to respect or kindness or education or self-determination.

Vela writes of language denied by sexist and racist and xenophobic institutions, by systems designed to enforce obedience rather than to spark and nourish consciousness. She writes of the many forces designed to warp and suppress the power of women and children, and the damage done by this misshaping. Those who accept themselves as mud are too soon ground to dust.

Vela also writes about speaking up, fighting back, demanding personhood in the face of all who would deny it. She writes about fear in the face of those who would crush her. She reveals the loneliness of following one's own path, all the while knowing the alternative is unthinkable. She writes about being an advocate to those who cannot speak for themselves.

Mireya Vela does not cast herself as exceptional. She reveals her flaws, her fears, her mistakes. She presents herself as a woman whose survival depended on not accepting the limitations she was expected to conform to. She writes about truth as a world-splitting weapon, one that can be wielded by any of us.

That's why, although the experiences Vela shares are raw with trauma, this collection of essays is never depressing. In fact, it is celebratory. Every word, this motherlode of language formed with loam and silt and clay, every breath, is a victory song against the forces that would keep us mute.

*Mireya S. Vela*

—Terry Wolverton, author of *Insurgent Muse: Life and Art at the Woman's Building*

# Introduction

MY PARENTS WERE IMMIGRANTS LIVING in El Monte when I was born in 1972. I spent all of my childhood and part of my adulthood living in El Monte. By the time I left, I had worked there as a teacher in multiple settings. Once gone, it never occurred to me that I would willingly go back. I always thought that if I returned it would be to dutifully visit my parents. So, in 2013 when I was called back to El Monte to do community work, I was initially devastated.

That's how trauma works. It makes you afraid of a place. All of the violence gets focused and concentrated until it's easier to think that it's a place that's evil and not the people who hurt you. But even thinking that someone, that a person, might be evil is reductivist. It reduces people to simple categories—tropes—and I hope that it's clear that these essays of my life are an exploration of things I do not understand.

But that is also how trauma works. It sends all the body's resources again and again to the same place, hoping for healing.

So, it's no surprise that I returned to El Monte. I had to work through nightmares and fears, but I arrived. When I looked into the audience, I hoped that none of my abusers were in the audience to crush me. But with or without them, I made a presentation on community research, asking community members to join me in an effort to become researchers themselves and ask questions. I wanted them to challenge the authority of their policy-makers, their leaders, their systems, their beliefs, themselves. And I did it with shaking hands.

They accepted our project. Together, we looked at all the data. I handed out a data deck so the people of El Monte could look at what the numbers said about their own city. The child abuse numbers in the city weren't surprising. Anyone who had lived there through child abuse knew that it felt like a lot. But seeing how El Monte compared to other cities was devastating. At the same time, community members were noticing that there wasn't enough childcare in the city. We collectively wondered how high child abuse rates and lack of childcare might be connected and whether we could leverage childcare to reduce child abuse. Could we use quality childcare to reduce child abuse?

We didn't solve abuse. But that was a critical time for me. It helped me to look at abuse head on—not as my personal abuse but on the concept of abuse and how it affects and impacts communities. With these women, I was able to own my abuse in another way. It was no longer this thing that had happened in dark moments of close contact, now it was a sickness. A sickness we could dissect and analyze. A sickness I might be able to understand.

These pages are my attempt at that. I try to look carefully at the systemic issues that played into my abuse. I try to look at the roles everyone had to play and why. I try to figure out why. Perhaps that's the trauma talking again, "Why me?" I try to be accountable here, too.

All accounts are the way I remember them. All accounts are a testament to survival. All accounts are a wild call to hope. I hope that others might join me in looking at abuse closely. I hope that others might save other children. But most importantly and selfishly, I hope these pages save me.

I am tired of drowning.

# Hiding in the Dark

BOULEVARD BENITO JUAREZ RUNS THROUGH the city of Tecate like an aorta. In the 1980s, it was the only paved street, connecting Tecate to major cities like Tijuana and Mexicali. My mother's family settled there over forty years ago after leaving California when jobs soured. Her brothers and sisters had come to the United States, following my grandmother and her ideas about opportunity. But when my grandmother returned to Mexico, her children followed, leaving my mother locked in her commitment to my dad.

The Serranos had felt separated from their people in El Monte, California. So, they all moved to the same street in Mexico in Colonia El Encanto. My grandmother lived on a large plot set amidst a wilderness, with little running water and temperamental electricity. Even there, especially there, humanity was at the mercy of nature and the animals surrounding them.

Next door, my tía was building her house. She and her daughter lived with my grandmother and grandfather while building crept forward. Two plots down, my uncle lived with his wife and two daughters. In the plot next to his, my divorced uncle lived with his grown son.

Mom married my father because she told him she would. The date she gave him was so far into the future, she thought he would lose interest and leave. But he didn't. When they wed, she married him because she believed in keeping her word. She always told me that a person was only as strong as their word. I doubt she was in love. I doubt she's ever been in love.

She woke up in the mornings at 5AM, made his breakfast and packed his lunch. She refilled his cup when it was empty. She stood near the stove to heat his tortillas, so they would always be warm when they reached him. But there was no kindness in their words. Their relationship was mostly

Our flashlight shone three feet ahead, illuminating dust flecks that twirled around us. We walked in the dark, tearing the night with our presence. The town was severely under built. Many homes didn't have running water or electricity or plumbing. Streetlights were stingily scattered. The natural darkness, barely broken by the human efforts in the town, loomed around us.

The orange dirt floated up as cars passed us from the unpaved curbside along our right side. It wasn't really a road, but cars ran wild here. We were all animals, the cars were simply constructed beasts made of metal parts and rubber bits. On our left, the cars rushed past the tar top of the boulevard. On our right, an incongruous emptiness expanded beyond my sight. Mostly, it was barren land. But in the distance, you could see the occasional shanty mutely lit with oil lamps.

I liked the emptiness. Not knowing what was out there meant filling that emptiness with my imagination. I saw people sitting around a table, telling stories of the past. Their future loomed uncertainly. But they retold the past with certainty, as if it was filled with facts instead of memories, and its people stayed fixed and beautiful. Even from afar, the shanties looked fragile. They were barely homes. People

5

enclosed themselves from the elements, while the beasts roamed the chaparral hoping to eat.

I liked imagining, instead. At home, my reality loomed with certainty. I was practiced at trying to disappear. If I pretended I was nothing, perhaps people wouldn't catch me with their gaze, and it would pass over your body without touching it. Like hungry uncles unsatisfied by wives. Like uncles too rabid with aberrant needs I didn't understand, but that made me feel a cold desolation.

The cars passing on our right picked up clouds of dust that clung to our shoes and clothes till we carried the land on us like a layer.

In the pitch dark, we couldn't see each other. I preferred the night around us, veiling me. My grandmother gripped my arm with her stiff, dry hands. In the dark, I could feel her shuffling stride, rhythmic and awkward as she pulled on me. Her back was curved like a nautilus. She stood barely at four foot, eleven inches. At 10 years of age, I was taller but she was the largest person I knew. She shone like a beautiful light. Her home was the cradle of my best childhood memories. For a few nights every four months, I felt safe in a way I couldn't at home.

My favorite person in the world was a hunchback, whose shirt strained against her back; who wore wedged high heeled sandals to feel taller; who couldn't sleep on her back; who was both made and diminished by the curving of her bones. I had no idea who she was before the deformity.

Nature isn't kind when it reshapes your framework. It pulled her in painful directions, forcing her downward and inward, readjusting her organs and stifling her breath.

Headlights tore through the darkness around us. Under the streetlamps, clumsy bats flew across to eat insects seduced by the lights.

Bats are a delicate species. They are sensitive to shifts in ecology. They need places to roost and areas to forage. Then, there is disease. Disease can ravage a colony of bats because of their tendency to live clustered together.

I've seen this, but not in bats. Behaviors, like disease, can ruin a colony.

In the dark, with bats flying overhead, surrounded by the chaparral of Mexico, I felt inconspicuous and unseen, like a bat. My grandmother and I walked a quarter mile before we turned around and walked back. There were two dirt roads that led to her home. We opted for the road furthest from us. That road had vicious dogs, likely asleep at that time of the night. We walked towards those dogs and away from the other road with the crazed woman who threw rocks at the people who passed. She would grow foamy with angst trying to protect her street. Her long skirts dragged. Dust coated her bare feet as she chased and yelled. Dogs were easier to handle. The language divide between us and the dogs protected us from the dog's insults. In contrast, the woman's curses vibrated though my body while I trembled.

Grandmother's home had a long driveway. I felt every step as we walked closer to her house. The toads seemed to wait for me to pass before they jumped across my path. I walked as confidently as possible, hoping the toads could not sense fear.

We entered the house through the back entrance, through the door that unlocked with a skeleton key. My grandmother walked in first as I followed. I looked out into the darkness before I entered. A wall of cactus grew 15 feet from the house. There was a chain link fence beyond the cacti. Beyond that chain link fence the land rose into hills, then rocks, then the chaparral where the untamed animals roamed.

Inside the house, my mom swarmed the kitchen with her sisters. They flitted about nervously like milky white moths—their skin as white and transparent as my grandmother's. Their arms powdered and veined in indigo lines. They rotated around my grandmother like I did. With my dark skin and dark thoughts, I felt separate. I wasn't like them. My opaque, olive skin was not a windowpane, displaying the mechanisms underneath. In fact, I hoped no one could see the things I hid within.

The tías fretted in high pitches that rang my ears. The air tightened. But grandmother ignored them. She moved around the kitchen cleaning and when she was done with the moths, she wandered into her bedroom.

Grandmother had migrated from her home in Zacatecas, to Mexicali, to Tecate. She had lived alone in California for 10 years. Borders seemed meaningless to her. She was dutiful and didn't complain. Perhaps, at that age you don't need to live outside yourself anymore. She'd lived across borders and outlived children. Had her pain caught at her throat and made her silent? My grandmother had made homes over and over again. She seemed to ground herself in the confidence of who she was. In this idea that wherever she was, that was home.

Before bed, we gathered around the table to eat sweet bread. The bakery was less than a mile away. They called themselves "El Mejor Pan." I bit down. My grandmother served me weak Nescafe. She sat at the table while I ate and the moths fluttered in the kitchen.

The next day, we traveled to Tijuana to visit my father's aunt and cousin. We returned to Tecate as night descended. The road back was winding and stark. My mother called this darkness "la boca del ogro" or the mouth of the ogre. My mother's imagination frightened me. In the dark, it was easy to imagine dark figures along the sides of the road. I shrunk further into the backseat and imagined what it might be like inside the mouth of an ogre. At what point would it swallow me? Had I already been swallowed?

We arrive in Tecate too late to do much. I'd missed an entire day of play with my cousins. I waited for my stomach to uncurl. I felt tight with anxiety and carsickness, but I was relieved to be back here.

Later, I lay on the wooden cover of the well. The well was fathomlessly deep. Uncovered, I was unable to see the bottom. Grandmother had thrown a bucket in. I had leaned forward as far as my courage allowed and caught the cold smells of the well. The bucket had splashed with an echo.

I wanted to reach more deeply. I wanted to touch the walls of the well that seemed to be covered in the moss as the well grew cavernous and blacker. How cold would the water be?

Covered, the well was a great spot for stargazing. The only light came from the house seventy feet behind us. My cousins and I watched for shooting stars. My vision was poor. I squinted and stared intently. Once I saw one, I'd make a wish.

I was relatively certain that my happiness was linked to how happy my mother felt. I wanted her to love me. I wished on the star for a cat, instead.

I wasn't ready to think then of how my mom was contributing to what was happening to me. One glance. What might it mean if she glanced away as those men cornered me? Would her courage leave her? I wasn't ready to consider how her choices might destroy me. Instead, I chose to believe what she told me, and pretend I didn't think she was lying when she said she loved me.

Occasionally, a breeze ruffled the leaves of the oak tree behind us. It was well known that there was a dead woman buried under that tree, with her baby. My cousins tell me that she was buried there incorrectly. I don't ask what that means. I imagined her buried bare, bent in an uncomfortable position, dirt rubbing on her skin, making her feel filthy. I knew what it's like to feel that dirty.

"We heard the baby cry a few nights ago," my cousin says. Sandra was my age but wise.

"Who else has heard it?" I said.

"Victor has heard it and Tío Manuel," she said.

Tío Manuel was the most intelligent man in our family. His words and experiences were serious business. He had seen many ghosts. When he felt generous, he did magic tricks for us and told us about the ghost that lived in his old house in Mexico City.

We left the well to play freeze tag underneath the street lights. The road was empty. Cars rarely passed through this area. Also, there were enough of us to warn if a car approached. If someone gave the call, we scattered to the side of the road, inhaling the dirt clouds the car left behind.

We ran. I loved and hated this. Though slow and unathletic, it was still thrilling to chase and be chased by other girls. Girls who acted like they loved me and never hurt me. I ran like I understood liberty of will. I ran as if I were free. I ran as if I wanted to be alive. I ran as if I understood safety. I ran as if I were carefree.

A few years later, I would start to cut myself. I would try to rub my skin off and burn my arms. I would sink into the hatred I felt for myself. Things would never feel like they felt during those moments, chasing other girls. At 10, I only felt the weight of shame. I didn't understand then that shame can turn. That shame can turn into itself and turn murderous. I didn't know that shame was only the beginning.

At our California home, I was the only girl. I was constantly outrun. I was constantly outmuscled. I outdid my brother and male cousins with my quick fists and mean words.

I was a feral creature there. Often hiding, often hunted.

I didn't know how to be gentle like my female cousins. I'd lived my short life hoping I drew first blood.

I ran until my lungs hurt.

The bats flew low and almost hit our heads. I felt the whip of their wings as they flapped.

That night, I stayed up as late as possible. My head filled with ghost stories and running. Eventually, I got tired and curled up on the floor next to my mom. I lay there staring into the pitch darkness, making out shapes on the ceiling till my eyes closed and morning arrived.

I woke to the sounds of tías washing the dishes and putting away food. They spoke loudly to each other, unaware or uncaring that I slept. I stumbled into the kitchen for breakfast, angry to be woken and ready to lash out.

Why did I need to do that? My anger boiled to the surface to burn me and filled me with shame. I hurt myself, and I hurt others. I needed to be outside where I could hide.

At home in California, I excelled at hiding. Lately I had been working on disappearing during the day. I worked on not being noticed. I worked on not mattering. I closed my eyes and wished myself so tiny, I wouldn't be seen. Self-hatred diminished me but couldn't make me disappear from the rabid eyes of the uncles trying to find me.

Eventually, we gathered in the small kitchen facing the hills. My tías talked about illness and husbands and scorpions and all the things that scared them. They'd built lives away from each other with their own families, but they wanted to be together. Their ideas were filled with fantasy and were as ungrounded as they were.

"Lili," Frencis said, "you can buy that plot of land on the corner. They are selling it."

"I don't know," my mother said, "I'd have to check in with El Viejo. I doubt he'd want to leave his mom."

"Maybe we can find him a job here and see if he'll consider it. You don't need a lot of money to get by here," Frencis said.

"Maybe," Mom said.

My heart filled with hope. I didn't initially know it was pretend. When I was 16, I ran away from home to be with my grandmother. I stayed there for weeks before my mother came back for me. To get me home, she promised me we'd move.

Thirty years later, she still lives in the same home, next to Grandmother and surrounded by uncles.

Back then, for the women, everything made more sense when they were clustered here. Together. Moths don't live clustered this way, but these women wanted to live piled together, looking like flowers, leaving their winged dust.

Bats cross the borders when needed. They don't respect human boundaries. Bats live all over Southern California. They go to where their needs take them, where they can find food and shelter.

I watched the moths and feared that I might swallow them whole with the evil inside me. My grandmother was home to me. She offered safety and love. When we left for the United States, I tried to hold on to what I had here. I tried to hold on to what this felt like. But I conceded. It's too dirty in that other house to keep my precious grandmother with me. I leave her and this feeling in Mexico, before I go back across the border.

The violence at home crowded my thoughts and squeezed everything out. At that house in California, the men in my dad's family were afflicted with a disease that made them crave children. They swallowed these children like the ogre swallowed us in the darkness. The disease was rampant. Our family was collapsing. And while I was easy prey, I refused to be a moth. I decided instead to be something altogether different. It's difficult not being able to choose to be a hunchback. I didn't have the years. I didn't have the experience, and the only child I had lost then was myself.

# Legacy of Rape

IN THE EARLY 1940S, IN a rural city in Mexico, my grandfather was arrested by the sight of my 16-year-old grandmother. She was stunning, with bright ribbons twisting her long braided hair. She wore the indigenous garb of the people in that region—embroidered blouses and skirts that caressed her ankles. She covered herself in rebozos.

I don't know much about what my grandfather did. I've heard stories about where he was from and what he did, but those stories are as fluid as the lies you tell children to get them to fall asleep. I know that one day with the help of friends, grandfather abducted and raped my grandmother, effectively claiming her as his own.

Bride abduction was a common practice there. It was barbaric. It was savage. It was romantic. A man wanted a woman so desperately that he took her for himself. He settled it with her family after the fact.

"He stole me," she said to me when I was 12, "I loved my home. I just wanted to be with my mom. I ran through the mountains to get away."

Her sandals moved the earth as she pounded her way through the hills, while her skirts moved and raised the powdered earth. The sounds of her breath were too loud, breaking through her throat, and coming between broken sobs.

She's never been a quiet woman. She's a woman that yells at the television during news and movies. She is loud and obnoxious passion.

He catches her by the braids and drags her to the ground.

She exclaims her emotions into the vastness of the mountains. Her cries echo, reverberating off the hills and back at her.

After he rapes her, she can't go home.

"Nobody wants you after that," she said to me.

She told me this story over and over even before I was a teen. It was as if she needed to relive it, control it, talk it out to banish it from her mind for a bit, so she could go back to curling her short hair—hair too tight on her scalp. She barely turned the spongy curlers once around each piece of hair. Hair too short to grab with a fist.

Grandmother was a violent staple in my life. Her feelings about that violence moved around her, like that dust that had covered the edges of her skirts.

The story about that night unraveled with each telling. Each time, the story became more lurid. It was a mass of violence and romance and violence. It was the beginning of a marriage. It was awful but not that bad. Fifty years into her marriage with my grandfather, she took responsibility for her vanity but wasn't sorry for it every time. She blamed herself for being beautiful or him for being an animal. She hated him. She loved him. He was the father of her children. He was hardworking and a good provider.

As the years progressed, her story folded me in. Where once it had been an experience my grandmother had gone through, it changed into something that would happen to me. Eventually.

I don't know how many siblings my grandmother had. They were reportedly cruel, hard people. I don't know how many men stole women or how many women were stolen by men.

I knew my grandfather was a rapist.

"My sister was stolen," she told me. "She was stolen by a group of men. When they had her alone, they flipped for her. They tossed a coin. That's how she ended up with the husband she has now. He was a really nice guy. She wouldn't have ended up with such a nice man otherwise. She was a mean woman."

If your father's mother is raped and your mother is raped and your aunts are raped, where does that leave you? The promise of rape looms.

One in five women will experience attempted or completed rape in their lifetimes. I wonder how many times these five women will be chronic victims of rape?

Before they became commonplace, her gifts of beautiful lingerie and switchblades confused me. She gave me a beautiful white enamel switchblade one year. I was 16.

"Stab between the ribs," she said.

She gave me a hatpin—a long needle I could make myself pretty with, but also use as a weapon.

"Stab them when they try to rape you."

When. That word caught between us. It became a promise.

Women are trained into this type of acceptance.

"Kiss your relatives."

"Hug creepy Uncle Manny."

"Don't be uppity. You're rude. Go sit on Uncle Joe's lap."

"Uncle Manny gave you a gift. Show proper gratitude."

"Liar. He didn't touch you. That's your imagination. Why are you always such a drama queen, looking for attention?"

Whittle down the women. Take off all the rough edges till they are smooth and fit into the palms of men.


My mother had her own technique.

"I'm cold."

"No, you're not."

"I'm hungry."

"No, you just ate."

"I feel sad."

"People like you don't feel sad."

To this day, I bristle uncomfortably when my experiences are invalidated.

Whittle the women down and fold them in. So that women know their place, their role. So their self never develops. So they are never individuals and never forget their legacy of service.

Perhaps that's what my grandmother was really telling me every time she gave me lingerie.

"I'm terrified of being raped," my mother told me. I'm in my early twenties and struggle to connect with her fear.

Who the hell gives a shit if another woman gets raped? We all get raped.

"I'm afraid to leave the house. It's my greatest fear."

I casually tell her, "No one is going to rape you, Mom. You are past the average age range to be raped."

"Old women get raped all the time."

"You have to stop watching the news. Those women with their boobs hanging out aren't journalists. They are eye candy with lies. That show isn't legitimate news."

In my mid-twenties, I'm a fifth grade teacher at an elementary school. I'm living in my hometown of El Monte, California, where the abuse rate is high and the domestic violence is, too. Housing is an issue. "A roof over your head" is loosely interpreted. People live in garages or on couches.

I'm struggling to meet the needs of my students. I'm struggling to take care of myself in this atmosphere. Every time I have to fill out an abuse report for the Department of Child and Family Services, I reel and need to vomit. When the cops come to pick up the kids, the children are always frightened. But I can't ignore the wire hanger welts on a child's skin.

One of my students is living with my uncle's girlfriend. We aren't directly related but that doesn't matter. They share four children. My uncle and his girlfriend don't live together. They are one of the reasons why the domestic violence in El Monte is so high.

Uncle's girlfriend and their shared children share a two-bedroom apartment with another family. This isn't surprising. Everything gets shared here. Everyone is just trying to get by.

Cousins share asthma inhalers. Mothers share medications. People share information or resources or gossip. Or whatever is needed.

One of the children in that shared household is my student.

One day, the girl tells me, "I heard from your grandmother that you are a whore."

The words come at me like the ground. I'm falling. Someone must have dragged me down by the hair.

"I'm not a whore," I say. My voice squeezes out from my throat. I sound pathetic and not credible. "I'm not a whore" is exactly what a whore would say.

I feel violated. I go home and tell my father. I ask him to please talk to his mother.

My mom says to me, "That's silly. You are overreacting. You know she doesn't mean it."

My father talks to his mom, but it doesn't matter. Her words hold true in her mind. This isn't the first time she's called me a whore and it won't be the last. The fact that I'm her only grandchild that went to college doesn't matter. The fact that I'm a respected person in the community doesn't matter. The fact that I work so hard to help families doesn't matter. I became a whore to her a long time ago. Perhaps it was my divorce or my newfangled ideas about feminism. Perhaps it's that she isn't sure whether that story she told me so many times was about her or about me. Or perhaps to her, we are all that woman running through the mountains, thick braids bouncing behind her, skirts tripping her progress.

# On the Bus

IN THIRD GRADE, THE BUS driver took a special interest in me. I climbed the bus in the morning, hoping that he wouldn't notice me. I crowded onto the bus with the other children on my street. In the mix, I must not have stood out. Or maybe he wasn't a morning person.

In the afternoon, I'd climb up the steep bus steps. I'd walk down the aisle looking for an inviting face to sit next to. Then, I'd find a seat alone among the cracked, green, pleather seats. I'd wait for an hour to get home.

At my stop, as I climbed off the bus, the bus driver threw an arm in front of me to stop me from leaving.

"Aren't you going to say bye to me this time? Maybe you can say, 'Have a good evening.'"

I froze. I was eight, but I knew what this meant. He wanted something from me. He wouldn't wait till I offered it.

The exit door stood wide open while he barred me from leaving. At the foot of the steps, my mom stood waiting. I didn't want to give him my words.

While the bus driver continued to tease me, she never spoke, never moved.

I mumble, "Good night."

"I can't hear you. Say it louder."

I become flooded with my own timidity and my Spanish mouth, trying to say those English words. I'd been taught to be polite. But this didn't feel right. It felt like a sick surrendering.

I glanced at my mom as she waited, cross-armed and silent. Even from the top of the steps, I could smell her anxiety and fear. I could tell her breaths were coming faster, like small hiccups. She held her small frame tight with her arms. Tight.

Tight like she had to hold herself up. Tight like her arms corseted her frame into place.

I wanted to protect her, while her passivity cut me like a knife. She never spoke up. Her fear caught in her throat like a scream, staring at me like she was watching an accident happen.

"Good night," I said more loudly, bending to give him what he wanted.

But I wouldn't make eye contact.

"That's good," he said.

I could feel him watching me as I reached my mother. She pretended she hadn't seen anything. She took my hand and politely thanked the bus driver. As I walked away, I felt the heaviness of his gaze.

With his eyes, he lifted my dress to see the stains on my underwear—and I let him.

The bus station was crowded with people carrying luggage and packages. One woman hauled two bulky boxes taped shut and tied tight with twine. They were likely treats and candies for the family she was visiting in the United States.

I traveled with my mom's sister. My aunt and I had one bag each. We were waiting for the bus that would take us from Mexico to the United States. I counted on my aunt to put us on the right bus. I dragged our bags into an enclosed part of the station, where it seemed safer.

I was 16 but she counted on me to keep her secure. In her fifties, she was prone to severe anxiety that racked her like seizures.

"Wait here," I said.

I gathered our bags and found her a place to sit. I was known for being tough, fearless. In the face of the anxieties quaking through the women in my family, the fact that I didn't break into hysterics was a major feat. They had decided I didn't have feelings.

"I'm going to see if I can spot our bus."

"Okay," she said.

I walked out, thinking she was safer inside, surrounded by a group of people. I pushed my way through to see what buses had arrived. I didn't see our bus. I walked back to check on her.

When I returned, a bony man was leaning on her shoulder. His slack mouth and unfocused gaze made him look almost delicate—like a newborn baby, surging forth from alcohol's womb. With his eyes waving back and forth between the back of his head and behind his lids, he didn't look prepared to make any decisions to hurt anyone. But Tía stared straight ahead, frozen as fear shook her body.

"What happened?" I asked.

I glared at the man. He was drunk and barely lifted his head. His eyes opened and closed but remained unfocused.

"Did this asshole do something to you?" I asked.

"He leaned on me and his head slid down my chest," she says.

She stifled a sob. I reached into my pocket.

"I haven't found our bus," I said.

I pulled out a pocket knife, a gift from my father's psychopathic mother who had filled my head with ideas of being raped.

As I opened the knife, the man slowly lifted his head.

"If this asshole leans on you again, stab the motherfucker."

We'd been speaking in Spanish. The drunk man initially ignored me, as he struggled to stay upright. But I stared at him intently as I gestured at him with the knife and handed it to my aunt.

He started a steady prayer, "No. No. No, no. No, no, nonononono."

It's a prayer I understood. It's the same prayer I used when my fears overtook me and I was trying to prevent feeling from escaping. He spilled off the chair and staggered away.

I went to find our bus. When I returned, Tía was still stiffly in her chair, shaking. With unsteady hands, she used the blade to clean underneath her nails. I almost laughed at her timidity, as well as her need to still behave like a well-bred lady.

I took the knife from her. I didn't feel the need to be a lady. My father's family had been calling me a whore for a long time and the word covered me like a crusted shell.

Abuse doesn't harden all of us. My aunt's husband had beaten her for 20 years and it seemed to have made her softer.

I stayed by her side the rest of the way home. Her fear drained her. She slept on the ride. I took the seat by the aisle, so she wouldn't be afraid. I didn't smile at others. I didn't invite conversation. I stared steadily forward, my eyes unfocused.

She would not have used that knife. But I wasn't like her. I couldn't think of a single thing I could possibly lose at that point in my life. So, I leaned back on the seat, as I tried not to feel anything but the courage of anger.

I liked riding in the back of the bus at age 21. The back seat has the benefit of a corner. I could sit there, lean to one side, and fall asleep.

The bus was nearly empty. I wrapped my arms around my backpack and pressed my items close to my pregnant belly. I dozed off.

I slept for 20 minutes—the distance between my college and the junior college closer to my home. When I opened my eyes, a man was seated next to me. The bus was full and standing students from the junior college crowded the aisles.

It was after 5PM on a weekday. It was the time when both students and employees left jobs and schools for home.

There was a biting cold in the bus, but at least it wasn't raining. When it rained, it always felt more crowded and the stifling smell of sweaty bodies and wet sweaters accosted the senses. The scent always reminded me of wet dogs.

I resettled my bulk and closed my eyes again.

I was visibly pregnant. But I was scrawny from months of vomiting. I was 20 lbs. lighter than I should have been.

I wore tights under a beige baby doll dress and brown Mary Janes. My hair was pulled back in a ponytail. I was blatantly aware that I looked like a kid, even though I was 21.

When I opened my eyes again, I saw that the man next to me had pulled out a switchblade. I looked closer at him. Like me, he appeared haggard and war torn. Unlike me, he hadn't taken the time to hide it behind a layer of make-up and a girly dress. He caressed the end of the blade with his finger as he talked to me or to himself or to the bus.

"Fucking pedophile. Fucking looking at little girls. I'm going to gut him if he looks at you again," he said.

I didn't respond. I looked at the man he was referring to. He was a kid—maybe 18 or 19 years old. He was tall and large with curved shoulders. His mass took up the entire aisle.

The kid looked at me. A lot of men did. It wasn't because I was pretty. My nose was fixed on my face like a large beak. My sour disposition was set on my mouth. But even with my eyes closed they could see into me. Men could tell I'd been abused. These men weren't even aware that this is what drew them to me. They wanted to know how "good" I was or how my flavor changed when I was vulnerable with fear or humiliation. The kid wanted to know if my eyes went soft like custard when pain racked my body. He saw me and reveled in the power of his maleness—and he wanted to know me better.

I thought, "Please don't look at me. Please don't look at me."

"He just has to look at you one more time, and I'll kill him," said the haggard man.

I wanted to tell him that I'm not a kid. I just looked like one. The man next to me continued to mutter and the kid continued to throw sideway glances my way, as I tightened with anxiety. Looking down at his knife, I saw simply that, a man with a blade. A knife is a knife. An angry person is an angry person. A protector protects. Sometimes that protection is aimed at you and sometimes it's not.

What was that kid thinking? Couldn't he see the blade?

The kid got off the bus before I did.

When my bus stop came, I stood up unsteadily and navigated my body down the steps and onto the sidewalk. The man with the blade rode the bus towards the bus station. I walked home.

I was owned by father before I was owned by my husband. I was property that had passed from my father's care into the hands of my husband. It had been like this for our women for decades. In rural Mexico, women walked with chaperones so they wouldn't be taken. We were a delicate group—fragile like the flowers in a field. We could be trampled. These old ideas reverberated within our system. Whenever I left the house, my family made it clear that outside was dangerous and that women belonged indoors. And they were partly right. Out in the world, the danger was public but naked. It had the stark rawness that could and would be witnessed. It was safer outside. Within the home, the abuse was silent and secret— unseen and unrecognized and hidden. So, I took my chances, out into the public, where I didn't have to live with the abuse under the same roof.

# Shoe Pilgrimage

IN 1981, THE SUMMER BEFORE I started fifth grade, my mom decided we needed to drive across the American-Mexican border to get shoes. Tecate is over 150 miles from where we lived in El Monte, California. To get there, we had to travel in the heat of June for three and a half hours.

That port, opened in 1919, is surrounded by vast expanses of land covered in brush and boulders and is one of three ports of entry from the San Diego region of California into Mexico. The border itself is a tiny break between the two countries. It's heavily guarded. While the Mexican patrol agents make a great show in their military gear and weaponry, it's the Americans you have to watch for. The Mexican patrol posture and bark at you, but the ease with which they let you enter their country says something about how they feel. The Americans, on the other hand, smile. But they take any opportunity to dismantle your car and humiliate you.

So, it was this divide of land and culture and false pretenses that separated my mother and I, despite the fact that we lived in the same city, in the same house, and spoke the same language.

That same border separated my mom from her own family—the family in Mexico, that made her so happy. The family that had birthed and shaped and raised her.

My mom's place in the United States always seemed tenuous—as if it were a temporary inconvenience before she packed up and returned to her own mother's house. Mom had never learned English or seemed to have adjusted to American culture. She didn't trust American doctors, or American officials, or American values.

Mom didn't trust American shoes either. She thought they wore out too quickly. She scoffed at the leather-like plastic throwaways so popular at the time. As a seamstress, she considered carefully the construction of shoes and clothes. She turned items over in her hands, looking closely at the seams. Mom didn't waste money on expendable items she thought should be an investment. If we bought shoes, they needed to last until the following year.

Mom started packing for Tecate the night before. We didn't have luggage. We packed our clothes, toys, blankets, and pillows into paper grocery bags. Trips to Tecate inevitably meant bags torn by pointed objects like toothbrushes and dolls. We packed pajamas, a change of clothes and towels. My hairbrush handle would rip through the bag and split it open. The tear would spread. Once gutted, the bag would release everything, bouncing out my dirty wares—pants, undies, tops—all those things that held together the seams of my budding womanhood.

And that bra. The bra I'd been carrying around. It was a hand-me-down from my cousin, Maggie, who was leaner and taller and had likely used the bra in the 4th grade. I would never fit into it. But I carried it as a flag to plant when breasts decided to emerge.

Other times, my dad would handle the bags roughly, seemingly blasé when our things spilled out of the bag and onto the floor to display my shrinking dignity.

The night before we traveled, I slept restlessly. In the morning, my mom would continue packing and fretting, unprepared to leave the house. She made sandwiches and sent my father out for last minute items like soda, or cookies, or chips. She checked the windows over and over and locked all the doors, as my dad yelled that we needed to leave.

Dad was proud of his car, a 1974 Impala he'd personally painted. He had a flair for choosing wild color combinations. This time it was a silver and lime green that gleamed under the sun. Each of the colors seemed to have an undercoat of glitter. There were Woody Woodpecker decals on the flanks of the car as flames shot out of the sides of Woody's mouth. My dad liked to think that this was because the car was burning rubber. He was going so fast that Woody spit fire with the intensity of dad's automotive speed.

Dad's mom stood by the chain link fence that separated our homes. I'd have to get close enough for her to touch me. With her right hand, she started by touching my forehead, then abdomen, and shoulders to form the sign of the cross. With that, our journey was blessed and we all climbed into the car.

Mom sat in the front next to my dad, in the bench seat that stretched from one side of the car to the other. My brother and I sat in the back. I always sat on the right behind my mom, and he sat to the left behind my dad. We piled the pillows and blankets between us. Eventually, we'd each use the pillows to sleep on. In the meantime, those pillows were vital in separating our spaces and keeping our rivalry at bay.

The trip started in a knot of stress that fluctuated throughout the journey. That stress was palpable in the back seat, while my dad berated mom for being slow.

"O, Viejo," she said.

"Ya sabias a qué horas me quería ir."

"Tenía mucho que hacer," she said.

"Siempre lo mismo contigo."

She spoke in a soft voice while he seethed and yelled. They were both in their thirties. But they used nicknames they'd given each other in the early years of their marriage. My mom responded with what I thought then was tolerance and patience but was instead a pattern of exhausted passivity.

Somehow, he always did it. He managed to suppress the violence he shook with. He eventually quieted to a grumble. He protested for the next 10 minutes, then his anger turned into heavy sighs. For the rest of the ride, Dad would rarely acknowledge we were in the backseat. Eventually, Mom would reach a hand behind to touch us gently.

Dad drove through El Monte and onto the 605 freeway in Whittier. My mom said a prayer as we entered the freeway. We drove south. It only took me about 30 minutes to fall asleep. There was a mechanical Coppertone billboard I loved. I tried to stay awake for it, but I didn't always make it. Up high, a little girl in blonde ponytails stood on the beach sand as a dog pulled her pants down again and again. She looked dismayed as her bottom was exposed by the aggressive, small dog.

I'd be asleep through Anaheim, Irvine, Dana Point, and San Clemente. Past San Ysidro my dad got onto the 805 and then the 905. He stopped once during the entire trip, about 45 minutes before we crossed the border to fill the tank with gas. We used the gas station bathrooms, while Mom stood outside watching for "bad men". Once in the car, we headed south again.

The curves were next. The final leg of the trip was filled with winding roads.

I hated being in a car for that long. I'm squirmy and dreamy, and I need something to do. Looking out the window entertained me but ultimately made me violently ill. A different sort of countdown started for me then. The roads wound and my dad hit the turns hard. My mom whimpered.

"¡Viejo, Viejo! No manejes tan rapido."

He laughed but slowed down for a while.

"Siempre tienes miedo."

My stomach turned with the curves. My gut hugged the edges of the road. In my mind, we tumbled down the embankment over and over again, just like my mom imagined aloud.

She compulsively did this, as if the anxiety filled every inch of her insides and needed to spill out into frightening words.

"No manejes tan rapido. ¡Viejo! ¡Viejo! ¡Viejo…! Vamos a chocar. ¡Viejo!"

Her whines grated on my mind. I couldn't figure out why my dad loved to rattle her. He eventually slowed down when we reached the border. He turned down the music, and I sat up straight. Usually, entering into Mexico, border patrol would simply wave us by. Relief would wash over me. In a few minutes, we would be at my grandma's house.

We drove down Bulevar Benito Juarez. This was the main road that went through Tecate. It was a wide road that cars sped through with two lanes going in both directions. People paused on the narrow island between the opposing lanes, before running across to the other side. This was one of the only paved roads in the town, so the dust rose on both sides of

El Bulevar, blocking our view of crossing pedestrians that dodged us as we dodged them.

We turned right off El Bulevar onto a dirt road, then right again onto Calle Primera, where my grandma lived. Elation hit me as I saw the gate. She had a long driveway, so I wouldn't see the house until we'd pass the gate. The gate was always locked. My mom got out of the car and walked the long driveway to the house to get a key.

My tía rushed out of the house once she saw my mom. My grandmother followed slowly, her severe osteoporosis affecting her pace. Eventually, she unlocked the padlock to let us in. My dad drove in and parked the car underneath the huge oak tree that shaded my grandma's home.

The Impala was a two door. My brother and I had to wait until the adults emptied the car and we were able to push the front seats to get out. I stumbled out. The nausea hadn't subsided and I felt dizzy. I hugged everyone and rushed to the bathroom. Behind me, my tía chatted desperately to my mother as she held her.

"Lidia. Lidia," she cooed.

Their voices like lullabies—sonorous in their love.

"Mireyita, Mireyita," my grandmother chanted as she wrapped her arms around me.

We walked inside as my tías asked my mom what she needed, and I found a place to lay down while my stomach settled.

In a few hours, we'd be back in the car, heading to the downtown area to shop for shoes.

Paved streets were strategically placed in Tecate. The downtown area was a hefty attempt at civilization. Most of the stores and homes within a half mile area had plumbing and electricity. Beyond that, homes spread out in rural isolation.

My dad parked the car and wandered away to the ice-cream and candy shops. Later, he would come back with bags of candy, bragging about the paletas he'd enjoyed. In the meantime, we hit the shops—Tres Hermanos, Trebo, Canada. The shopkeepers displayed their shoes in large windows. Each pair of shoes was displayed to show the front and the side.

Women's shoes were on one side and men's shoes on the other. There were no pink shoes here. All the shoes were black or brown, with the occasional white shoes meant for christenings or catechisms. When you knew what shoes you wanted, you went inside. A shopkeeper would follow you out and you would point to the shoes you wanted. But we weren't there yet. It would still be about 3 hours before my mom settled on a pair of shoes.

Mom considered the shoes carefully. She didn't want shoes that were flimsy looking, but she also needed the shoes to be somewhat feminine—in that thick rubber sole, even Frankenstein can be feminine. In the June heat, we shopped all the shoe stores on one side of the downtown area, before we jaywalked to look at all the shops on the other side.

On each side, the sidewalks were lined with men ready to catcall the women. Without Dad, Mom was suddenly an available woman. She had unusual coloring for a Latina. Her hair was light brown and her eyes almost green. Her skin was milky—and her shyness was like a dare to touch her. The men stood straighter as she passed and mumbled words of praise and longing.

"Remember what shoes you want," she said.

"Okay," I said.

"The black shoes you liked were from the Tres Hermanos next to the park. Let's go to the Tres Hermanos across the street. Maybe they will have other shoes there."

Once we had reviewed all the shops, we both tried to remember the location of those evasive perfect black shoes we had spotted five or six stores ago—on the east side of the street or the west. My mother was fastidious, and getting the right shoes was a long negotiation where I subdued my needs and agreed with her as she ruminated on the "right" shoes and doubted herself in long circulating thoughts.

The shoes we finally bought were one size too big and blistered my feet. Eventually, they would be too small and press my feet tight, until my right toe ate through the leather.

We would leave for home on Sunday. The ride home was grueling. The wait to cross the border back into the United States took about two hours as the border control agents scrutinized who to allow through.

This part was always hard for my both my parents. My father tried hard to smile and appear friendly through his severe anxiety. My mom handled and mishandled and dropped the green cards. Then, my dad would step out of the car as the agents had him open our truck to look through our things. From the back seat, I could hear them rummaging through our bags as my father politely said "Nothing" and "Thank you".

Once he was back in the driver's seat, the agents looked at my brother and me, and asked us for our papers. We mumbled "American citizen" with our bilingual mouths. Our tongues had been making Spanish words and at the sudden request for English, I stumbled over the words, trying to make them sound American.

On Monday, I would wear my Frankenshoes to school. The weight was unfamiliar and it would take days for them to feel right. For the next year or so, I would wear the shoes under every condition—church, school, parties. To my mortification, I would wear those shoes to PE.

During kickball, I'd drag my Frankenshoes towards the ball, hoping to make contact. On those rare occasions when my thick shoes touched the ball, I could feel my ankle bend under the weight of the shoe. Ultimately, it would be the top of my foot that would sweep the ball towards the field. The effort was monumental and the fight against gravity was an effort that was rarely rewarding. I lumbered towards first base but rarely got there safely.

While my friends wore their pink, patent leather Mary Janes, or sneakers that matched their outfits, I would wear the thick soled, stiff, leather shoes, polishing away the scuffs and tears as the months wore them down. It would be another year or two before I felt shame and anger about the shoes. My parents worked hard and expected us to be grateful. After all, having the money to buy shoes is a matter of pride. Even if your shoes are ugly.

# Hypnagogia

IN 1981, I DESPERATELY WANT a Sea Wee doll. In the commercials, a delicate girl plays in a bubble filled bathtub while her mom kneels alongside her. I want that. I want to be in a bathtub and feel the safety of the water and the tickle of bubbles while my mermaid dolls floats in a sponge lily pad, and my mom lovingly hovers. I'm eight years old. I want my nudity to stop being the dirty thing it has become. I want to be safe.

"What would you do if you got one?" Mom asks.

"I'd kiss that person and give them a big hug," I say. This is unusual for me. I don't like to be touched.

"Really?" she says. Her voice is creeping.

"Yes."

"Are you sure?" she says.

Her words are like a sharp grab and I feel unsteady.

"Yes," I say.

On Christmas Eve, I open a gift with the doll in it. It's from my father's youngest brother, whose persistent stare terrifies me. I don't touch him or thank him. Instead, I'm overwhelmed with the feeling that I just bartered something. It feels sickening.

My dad's youngest brother hates me into my twenties.

Standing on the church steps for wedding photos, I see the angry veins on his face. I'm a bridesmaid at my brother's wedding; I'm wearing a red, strapless dress that makes me feel vulnerable and naked. Over the dress, I'm wearing old shame like a threadbare coat.

He's a pastor and has just married my brother to his new bride.

I hear the photographer tell us to smile. He's posed us while the pastor watches. The happy couple are at the center while the bridesmaids flank from above and the sides.

"Mireya," the pastor's voice booms over the shuffle of dresses.

"You're up high right now. I bet you really like that," he says, "but don't for one second think you are better than anyone here."

I've cried throughout the ceremony. It feels like I'm losing my brother. I turn to the pastor's voice but I keep my gaze at his shoes. I imagine the robes flapping, his teeth long and perspiring—the froth forming at the corners of his mouth. I look up and he is simply glaring at me. But in my imagination, he's trying to consume me.

He is arrested in 2006. To evade police, he drives from his home in Sunland to his mother's house in El Monte—next door to the house where I grew up. The newspaper headlines read "Pastor and Son Arrested on Charges of Child Molestation".

After the arrest I realize that in his mind, I somehow twisted his lust. I was a two year old, or a six year old, or a ten year old, with the power to move him away from god. He'd molested the girls in his church. He'd molested the girls in our family into their teens.

As an adult, when I wake up from nightmares, I take quick stock of my surroundings. My biggest fear at that moment of wakeful confusion is that I will open my eyes and see the beige door to my room at my mother's house. I look for the windows and sense the tightness of the air. It always takes me a moment to realize I'm safe. I reach for my husband. If I'm able to touch him, my alarm diffuses. If he's not there, I listen for the sounds of his feet upstairs.

In that moment, when I am stuck between awareness and the pull of the dream, I'm terrified. I wouldn't relive my childhood for anything in the world. My creativity is born in the imagination, a space that is so much like hypnagogia, it's likely the two are married. I am working to accept this space in my mind where ideas, both good and bad, float like butterflies. I don't own that space. It's where all artists go. It's where girls sit in bathtubs with mermaid dolls imagining safety and a mother who watches over them.

That moment between the creations of the imagination and the awakeness of reality, that's where I'm stuck for him as well. That's where I live. I'm not alone there. It's also a place for pastors.

# Rules of Being a Woman: Conventions and Following Lies

MY MOTHER SAID TO ME, "Girls are pretty and delicate like flowers. They need to be protected."

"What about boys?" I asked.

"Boys are not like that," she said.

"Then what are they like?"

She wouldn't answer the question. Instead she said, "Don't be like your father. He is very rough, impatient, and bad tempered. You need to be polite and patient and giving.

Always speak with kindness. You need to learn from what I tell you, not from what you see."

I was 10 and all around me I saw violence. There were those that crushed and those that got crushed. I didn't want to be crushed. I didn't want to be delicate. I didn't want to wear pink dresses with matching tights. I wanted to be upside down and chase animals. I wanted to play in the dirt and sweat like a beast. I wanted to be wild. I wanted to explore. I wanted to read books and discover new things. And all of these things, were against the limitations my family had set on women.

I went to college despite a conversation I overheard between my father and his brother. As I was rounding the hallway into the living room, I heard my name and stopped.

"Are you seriously going to let her go to college?" Uncle asked.

"She's been accepted," Dad said.

"Education is wasted on a woman. You'll pay all that money, and she'll end up knocked up and married. Why educate her if she'll just end up at home raising children?"

"She wants to go," Dad said.

"She's going to end up with *ideas.*"

"Yeah. Yeah. I know. She's so stubborn," Dad said.

The knots in my stomach twisted. I made some noise as I entered the living room to announce myself. They stood cross armed, facing each other, as they decided on my life. They barely knew I was there.

Human beings are social animals. We have evolved to survive together as a group. Alone, we don't do as well. Because of this need that makes us depend on one another, we have also developed the social skills to bend, forgive, and accommodate others. People have adapted to form unions and stay together.

My father is the eldest brother in the family. I was the second eldest of the grandchildren. The eldest, a male cousin, was sporadically attending junior college. I had applied to a private college and been accepted. While my male cousin struggled to figure out what he wanted to do, I declared my major. He dropped out before I graduated.

A "good" woman, in my family, knew how to do two things: she didn't question, and she followed conventions. That is their role as people who will pass down the culture and the language. The culture had taught them to buy into the bullshit. They believed the lies and kept their mouths quiet. But most importantly, they never suggested to the men that they might be smarter.

My mother stayed close when my father ate. Sometimes, she ate with him, but mostly, she stood in the kitchen to heat his tortillas. She flipped them back and forth as she asked about his day. I don't ever remember him asking about hers.

He didn't like to eat cold tortillas, so she watched him, delivering hot ones as he finished the previous one. When his drink ran out, he wanted his cup refilled quickly.

She wasn't allowed to complain or disagree or be her own person. She was his property. She didn't see her family or friends unless he said it was okay. She asked for permission.

But most importantly, he treated her as if she were extremely stupid.

College is already difficult when you are the first woman in your family who has decided to attend. It's even harder when you're alone in your decision. There were days when my dad seemed proud of my decision to go. He thought that if I was going to college, it was his accomplishment. He liked the idea of having a kid in college. But it wasn't always like this. Most days, he didn't like what college meant for me. He didn't like the reality of what college might mean for him.

In Mexico, I'm in the kitchen flipping tortillas. I'm still in college and my dad is bragging in the other room.

"Sherlock Holmes is the best detective that ever lived. I bet you don't know who he is," he told one of my aunts.

"I don't know. Say the name again," she said.

She's dusting off and cleaning the table. She picks up the dishes on the table.

"Sherlock Holmes. God, I can't believe you haven't heard of him. He's everywhere. How can you not know this?" he said.

"I don't know. He sounds familiar."

From the kitchen, I call out, "He wasn't alive. He was a fictional character."

"What? Who the fuck asked you what you thought? Shut up."

My aunt froze and threw me a silencing stare. I thought I was quietly informing and teaching. Instead, I had unmanned him. I was destroying his perceptions and flattening his world.

We were in Mexico, where dad was on his best behavior. He usually puffed his chest big and stood in front of me, roaring, while I feared he would strike me. He'd yell, "Shut up or I'll break your teeth in."

In Mexico, he was restrained. He puffed up but he did not push into my space until I cowered.

I've always thought of evolution as happening slowly. Fish don't decide to simply walk out of the water to live on land.

My family thought my self-concept too lofty and my plans too ambitious. I was reaching for too much. I wasn't delicate. I wasn't feminine. I wasn't polite. I no longer asked for permission to cut my hair. I didn't look down when my superiors spoke to me.

What's worse, I'd been accepted into this new overture into American life. This wasn't ours. Our rites of passage included Baptisms, First Communions, Confirmation, and Quinceñeras. Rites of passage that included a trip to church, where girls reaffirmed their connection with god and their willingness to behave and obey the patriarchy.

Grandmother thought only whores went to college. In college, outside the constraints of the family, women became lusty animals looking for opportunities to have sex with as many men as possible. Without family and guidance, we were rabid creatures of unmollified lust. Each one of us—including her granddaughters—were whores in the making.

Usually, the lewdest talk coming from my grandmother's house didn't reach me, but a few days after my father had that conversation with his brother, a cousin approached me.

I wanted to attend college and everyone had an opinion. It was such a vigorous discussion within the family that it spilled outside the confines of my grandmother's home, over the fence that divided our homes, into our home, and into my awareness.

Apparently, they had all voted me down. They had envisioned my future, planned what they wanted for me, and it didn't include college.

"No one thinks you should go to college," this cousin said.

He was a distant cousin, the child of my grandmother's sister's children. He had intense eyes and was rumored to have a bad temper. He was short and always neatly dressed; in dress pants and a dress shirt. It was a Sunday, and he'd just come from church.

"But I support you," the cousin continued, "I think you should get educated so you can homeschool your children."

I opened my mouth to respond. I didn't want children. I didn't want a husband. I opened my mouth and closed it, like a fish struggling to breathe.

I ignored the will of the group. They continued to talk about me. But when I decided to go to college, my mother stopped talking to me. She had an odd relationship with my father's family. My father's mom must have talked to her about what they thought. She had conceded. Concession is what Mom did best.

She wrapped herself in leaden silence. My mom had given me the choice of two schools to attend. I pulled out a map and she had chosen the schools I could apply to based on proximity. I'd filled out all applications on my own. I don't think she'd expected me to get accepted.

I wasn't the type of daughter she was. I don't think she ever did anything that separated her from her family. I wondered if she had a sense of self. She'd listened to her own mother's opinions as if they were words being brought down from the mount. Grandmother Lupe had decided when mom would stay in Mexico and when to move to the United States. Mom had followed the advice, despite not wanting to leave her home in Mexico. Grandmother Lupe had also decided whom my mom should marry. Before my father had courted my mother, his brother had asked to date her. Grandmother Lupe had refused him. My father pursued my mom with Grandmother's approval.

Grandmother Lupe set the rules. She set the rules for marriage. She set the rules for how children were raised and how religious beliefs were followed. And because everyone was afraid to displease Grandmother, the women stayed married to the husbands they frequently viewed with bitterness, distaste, or fear. These men might hurt them, or beat them, or cheat on them, but god's word was law and couples couldn't break a union created by god.

I wasn't like my mom, who understood her place in the hierarchy these other mothers had created. I had the strong will of both my grandmothers. I couldn't suspend my own ideas and thoughts to subject myself to the rules of another person. I tried. But again and again, my own will surfaced. This made me, mom said, "Una hija mala."

Mom stopped talking to me for three months. I walked around her, over her, against her. I waited for her to accept my decision.

When months passed and that didn't seem likely, I worked on how to accept my status as the person in the family that no one talked to.

My parents had not allowed me to live in the dorm. Instead, I took the bus to and from school. Many women in our family didn't drive and my dad had refused to teach me.

Mom grounded herself in tradition, in family, and leaned hard on the word of god. She was a woman of established patterns. She trusted the things she felt. These feelings were messages god sent her, as he responded to her anxieties and prayers. She leaned towards her premonitions and listened for the voice of the divine.

In the morning, I got up early to catch the bus. I rode the bus the forty-five minutes it took to get to school. At school, I felt out of place. I worked hard, then made the trip back home, where no one would speak to me.

"Go to bed," she said, once she'd started talking to me again. Her mantra began at 9PM.

"Go to bed," she said.

"I'm studying. I've got to finish this."

"You always sleep so late, and you keep the rest of us up," she said.

"I'm trying to be very quiet," I said.

"Go to bed."

"Mom, this is college. This isn't like high school," I said.

"But I know you're awake and that keeps me awake," she said, "I need to know you are in bed like the rest of us."

I studied hard to keep up with my peers. I stayed up to keep up with the demands of my professors. I was studying literature—and in the back of my head, I was deathly aware that English was my second language.

"Don't you care about anyone but yourself? You know I wake up early," she said.

"Why are you doing this to your mother?" my father said.

"I'm trying! I'm trying!" and even though the high pitch didn't reach my outside voice, I could feel the combination of isolation and alienation working inside me until there was a high pitch that didn't ease.

The next day, it started over again.

Mom couldn't fathom college.

"When you talk," she asked, "aren't you afraid people will think you are stupid?"

"Um, no...."

But I was afraid. I didn't come from privilege and the collective intelligence that's built into a family when parents have surpassed a third grade education and go to museums. I came from poverty, where every day was a potential day I might not make it. I came from a neighborhood filled with gangs, rape, drugs, and violence.

I likely didn't have anything valuable to contribute to the college discussions. But I didn't care. I wanted my voice to be heard—whether or not it was smart or shook with terror.

I became adept at falling asleep almost anywhere. With the sleeplessness catching up to me, I began to sleep in the school library, on campus under trees, on the bus, and at the park. At the park, I gathered myself small and rolled my jacket into a pillow. I hugged my backpack and slept while hearing the children nearby screaming the joys of freedom that come with play and chase.

Lying there in the grass, I felt homeless. This was a feeling that would stick with me for 10 more years, no matter where I lived.

Mom thought that in college I was becoming a hard, logical woman with liberal ideas. She could see, as I could see, that my education was driving a wedge between us. She panicked as I practiced what it meant for me to be a person instead of a daughter.

I was on this road of being a person on my own, with no guide, and no one to speak to.

There is nothing more painful than being alone when you desperately don't want to be. Connecting to others fulfills some of our most basic needs.

I found company in books. I'd lost my soul to them years before. Within them, I escaped my home life. I spent hours in the worlds writers created. There, I felt validated. I felt understood. Just as mom's religion wouldn't bend, mine stayed just as steady. I wouldn't have been able to change directions even if I'd wanted to.

Neuropsychologists have found that social rejection is experienced like physical pain. Lack of relationships is closely linked to depression.

Our home was separated from my dad's mom by a chain link fence. During the second year of college, one of my dad's younger brothers approached me.

"I heard you have money," he said.

"I don't have money."

"I need to borrow some cash. You've got a grant for college, right?" he said.

"Yes, but I can't spend that. It's for college."

"Let me borrow some. It's for something important."

"No."

"You're such a selfish bitch," he said to me, as he walked away.

"Yes," I said, "I know."

In ancient societies, ostracizing was used as a form of punishment. Being thrown out of the group that you belonged to was considered worse than death.

I got pregnant during my junior year in college. For all my work, I ended up pregnant at an age only a year later than my mother had been pregnant with me.

I thought I was working against beliefs, against trends, against the grain. Yet, here I was in the same place my mom had been twenty years before me. In some ways, I took pride in not having become a teenage pregnancy like the women and men in my family had predicted.

But here I was in the same place they'd been at my age.

In the morning and in the afternoon and in the evening, I fell on my knees and mouthed a mantra of hope, "Please...please...please
...please..." as my stomach emptied into the toilet.

My "new" ideas bent to the stresses of a pregnant body. Like my mother and her mother and her mother before her—

like all the women I knew, the baby in my body took over. I bent towards motherhood. I kept the baby.

I took my pregnant body to school with me. This created a much bigger divide between myself and the students at the campus, whose parents sent them to Paris for their birthdays.

As before, I climbed on that bus in the morning and went home in the evening exhausted.

My mom, of course, was furious that I was pregnant before marriage. So, I got married. I took some time off when the baby was born, then went back to school. It took me two years to finish that last year.

As I finished my last year, both my parents and husband discouraged me and ranted about how I was unwilling to put the baby first.

I was. I was thinking long term.

I have often wondered what it would have been like to maintain tradition, stay at home 'til a man noticed me, married me and we had children. I have often been sorry I went to college.

It took me 10 more years to separate and build my own family. For 10 years, I roamed without ties or roots. For years, I was desperately lonely.

It's an asset to be a major disappointment to your parents. Once people's expectations are that low, you get to rewrite your own role. There's power in being a pariah. There's power in disappointing. There's power in breaking the rules.

But there is pain, too. And the loneliness is stifling.

Being thrown out of your tribe also helps to protect that group's social norms. Ostracism helps to protect that group's beliefs and social values. It protects that group's identity.

I'm in my forties now, and have gone back to school again and again. I like learning and I still love books. Mom calls me when she hasn't heard from me in a while. Personally, I enjoy our long silences. The chasm between us is a known and comforting factor.

Mom doesn't prefer the facts. On the phone, she calls me jovially. She pretends I didn't run away from home repeatedly. She pretends she never ostracized me or manipulated me or hated me. She and I both pretend that all of these things didn't break me. But mostly, she pretends she didn't betray me at every turn. On the phone, we are old friends greeting each other, trying to catch up.

On the phone, she pretends to love me, and I don't argue.

She likes things this way. I'm married to someone she likes, I have children, I have my own home. On the surface, I'm everything she ever wanted.

"How are the kids?" she says.

"Good. The kids are fine."

"And Dan? How's he doing?" she says.

"Really well," I say.

"And how is Raquel's mom?" she says.

It's her wording that always reminds me who she is, who I am, what we created between us. She chooses words that don't acknowledge me as a separate woman—as a full person who can stand alone. She doesn't ask me about work. She doesn't ask me about my advocacy work or my volunteer work. She doesn't know what I do for a living.

"I'm fine. How are you guys doing?"

"Good," she says.

With the script done, she hangs up. She's reminded me she's there and that I'm here. I feel the pain of knowing that it isn't me she's talking to. On the phone, I'm the daughter she always wanted. But I'm also this thing she can relate to; I'm a mom. I'm a role. Within that I'm a known quantity, not this whole other thing that refused to follow her rules and bulldozed her way out of the family.

Mom and Dad are the only people that talk to me. And that's fine. The absence of an extended family reminds me of my choices. It reminds me of how much I felt I was worth. Each time I think about them, I regret everything. The best I can hope for is that they also think about me and feel regret, too.

I burned a trail through that family. I rewrote the rules. I know my mom isn't proud of my accomplishments, but my father's eyes gleam when I talk about them. I know he goes back and brags to his mom. This makes me wonder about that moment when I was 18 and walking down that hall, what my father was really saying and thinking. And what exactly it meant when he didn't encourage my defiance, but also didn't discourage it. I remember what he said, but I also remember what he didn't say. He never told me to decline the acceptance letter to college. Did he gleam then, too? Did he think about how this might rewrite his life and the decisions he had made? Did he regret wanting to break my teeth in at least once a day? Did he regret his daughter?

My own daughter shocks me. She's bold and says things that are amazing and smart and funny. She's creating her own trail. I thought I knew what it meant to rewrite things and redefine what it meant to be a woman. I thought my ideas were progressive. But here she is, teaching me otherwise. She's got adventure in her blood like I did. I encourage her to flex her power and try new things. I don't tell her what girls and woman are supposed to be. Instead, I stand back to listen, hoping to learn things that are new.

# Doctores

GRANDMOTHER DIDN'T LIKE SECRETS. SHE said to me, "Secrets come from Satan." I don't know if she really believed this, or if she liked the power as she hissed it in my ear.

She was devastating to be around. I kept an eye on her hands—fidgeting or violent. She wanted my most intimate thoughts and secrets, she dug in with her words. Are you having sex? No, too young? Are you letting the boys at school look at your panties? Do other girls do that? No? You think you're so smart. Better than me, huh? You're not going to feel so smart when you are 15 and pregnant. All that education won't mean anything when your husband beats you up. You'll deserve it. Someone has to beat your opinions out of you.

In her youth, she had been beautiful. In a painting commissioned by one of her sons, she's striking in a traditional, embroidered top. Her hair is plaited into thick ropes, looped and tied with green ribbons. Her stare is direct and emotionless.

In photos yellowed with age, she's a squat overweight woman staring into the camera, unaware that she has degenerated. She's tightly bound with girdles and corsets. Legs were encased in support hose. Her body was sausaged into polyester muumuus. On her ears, she wore traditional Mexican earrings shaped like birds with tails dangling into teardrops. The gold in her ears matched the gold partials in her mouth.

But if she was feeling mean, she took them out to make you hold her teeth.

In her practice as the local healer, she didn't offer operations or invasive measures, but she was what the neighborhood of El Monte had available if they couldn't go to American doctors. She had herbs and syringes. To those people, she was a relief. Poverty is an amazing stressor. While mainstream people can go to doctors or even a free clinic, marginalized people have to find alternative methods to cope.

There's scant money, and if families are also undocumented, this takes its toll in fear and anxiety. Most often, families use illegally prescribed drugs, expired drugs, or drugs other family members discarded or didn't use. They also buy drugs at the Swap Meet.

Our diseases are different, too. American doctors don't understand what it meant to suffer from bilis or susto or latido. These are constructs from a different country, from a different world, from a different time. So, the women came to my grandmother instead, hoping she might help them. They brought their vials to her. For a few dollars, she patched them up and pushed them onward.

> *Rosemary can be used for a number of things. It can help with stomach problems and for blood circulation. To reap the benefits, you boil the stems with leaves in water until the water turns an avocado green. You drink it. It tastes like bitter moss water. You need to drink lots of it for long periods of time for it to work. Because of the amounts you will have to consume, it's best to have a plant—and a bathroom nearby. You*

*can also boil rosemary and put it in your bath*
*for muscle pain.*

The herbs grew at the perimeter of the yard behind the chain link fencing that surrounded her house. My grandfather kept a chain wrapped around the double gate that closed with a spring lobster clasp. A non-working metal padlock hung on one end to make people think the gate was secure. The chain and lock didn't impede anyone. Men could easily jump onto the chain link fence, plant a foot over the top while their arms supported their weight and leap over. But that metal padlock comforted my grandmother.

The two women stood outside the gate and banged the loose end of the chain against the gate. Metal clanged against metal. Loud and obnoxious.

"¡Doña! ¡Doña!" called the older woman.

They took a few steps back when the dogs charged the fence, rabid with excitement. Grandfather gripped his knees and heaved himself to his feet.

"¡Sáquense!" he said. He kicked the dogs away.

Grandmother inched the living room curtain to watch. She lowered the loud TV volume. Grandfather unlatched the chain.

"Pásense," he said.

The women came into the yard. The one holding the baby gripped the child closer. The baby was wrapped in many blankets to prevent the air from hitting his face.

Had the women looked up, they would have seen Grandmother peering from the curtain. My grandmother glared at how closely Grandfather stood next to the women and how widely he smiled. She grumbled, ready to battle her claim over him.

"Animál," she said to the empty room.

With her tongue, she adjusted the partials and bit them into place. She stood by the heavy iron door to greet the women.

"¿Qué quieren? ¿Qué tiene el niño?"

"Fíjese que no se siente bien. Llora mucho," said the older woman.

"Vamos a ver que tiene."

Grandfather got back on his knees to continue weeding, while my grandmother led the women inside; they took a seat. The mother peeled the blankets away from the baby. The baby emerged from the blankets dazed.

The women sat and began to explain the baby's symptoms to her.

Those neighborhood women sought Grandmother for her medicinal wisdom. She could look at a child and tell whether it needed to be healed from a susto—a fear. She used corn oil or lard to cook, but kept a bottle of olive oil for customers. She rubbed the baby joints so deeply her thumbs squeezed through to the bone. Her squat, thick hands massaged the temples, holding the bridge of the tiny nose in one hand and the nape of the neck in the other, pulling up, as the baby wailed in pain. She cooed and worked and gave them oil to drink. Children left her home slick as seals after an oil spill and just as alert.

*Tomatoes soaked in alcohol can be tied with*
*rags to the feet of toddlers and young children*
*to bring down a fever. However, the child will*

*be extra unhappy at having to do this. The
tomatoes do not feel good. They are squishy and
cold. The tomatoes feel even worse when they
have warmed up and their seeds have traveled.
The child will look back and become angry
every time they think about it.*

Women came for their needs, too. They came shyly or
insistently, handing my grandmother the tiny vials filled with
clear fluids they smuggled from Mexico, clear as water but
bitterly fragrant. My grandmother took the syringes from
their place behind the locked vitrine. While the women waited,
my grandmother boiled the needles and syringes in her
kitchen till the glass turned opaque, then pulled them out with
the tongs she used to flip tortillas. Needles were not easy to
obtain. She reused the same needles, blunt with overuse. Their
sharp points rounded, causing more pain as they pierced
through the flesh and into the muscle.

She took those vials without understanding what was in
them. Even in her late sixties, my grandmother was barely
literate. She could write her name and read falteringly, but
rarely remembered how to spell my name or any of her
grandchildren's. Her family did not think girls were worth

educating. She'd carried that belief along with her when she'd migrated. She'd moved across into another country but she'd brought all of her beliefs with her, never conforming and never blunting her sharp edges.

When Grandmother was ready, the women followed her to the back room where they lay on her bed face down. The middle of her bed sagged where the springs had bent from my grandparents' weight. The room was filled with perfumes and lotions. The mirror in her bedroom was dull from the loose Avon talc powder she applied every morning. The large containers were sealed with thin rice paper that barely contained the clouds of white that burst forth when she released the enormous pouf to powder her neck and breasts. On the corner of her dresser sat a wig from the sixties on a red velvet Styrofoam bed. On occasion, Grandmother would hold the wig upright with her left hand while she brushed it like a cat.

In her bedroom, the women lay on their tummies, undid zippers, and pulled down the back of their pants to reveal pale orbs. They squirmed and shut their eyes, as Grandmother climbed into bed with them; her enormous weight tipped the bed as she crawled across the space. She breathed raggedly as she positioned herself above the woman. She felt the muscle, pressing, as if tenderizing the meat. She cleaned the woman's flesh with a cotton ball soaked in alcohol. She dipped the vial, sucking the stuff into the syringe. She pushed the plunger till the liquid squirted and the needle was clear of air. With a quick flip of the wrist, she impaled their flesh, injecting the fluid into their muscle, then rubbing the injection site vigorously with her naked fingers.

The woman limped back. On leaving, she handed Grandmother a few crumpled dollars. Did she feel my grandmother's hatred, heavy as the demons Grandmother tried so hard to keep out of her home? She spoke poorly of these women who came to her with their bare buttocks and their naked need, their children wrapped tightly in blankets.

> *A red thread must be used during an eclipse to protect a pregnant woman. This is especially important if she refuses to wear the red underwear her grandmother is sure she gave her last Christmas. The thread protects the baby from the harmful effects of the eclipse, which can cause birth defects. While this may seem unlikely, red thread acts as a force field.*

"She's on birth control," Grandmother said. "Who knows who she's fucking? She's not even married."

"Look at her," she said. "See how she twists her body when she walks? What a whore."

They trusted her with their vials and their secrets and their children. Did they know she couldn't read what was on those tiny bottles they handed her? Those medicines, smuggled dangerously across countries, were so precious. Could they read her vacant eyes, blurred by a layer of cataracts? Those eyes, which were so eager to know their ailments and gaze at their naked vulnerability? She rolled her partials in her mouth with her tongue as she delighted in their misfortunes.

*Saliva is of vital importance if you want beautiful skin. In particular, it helps with acne. To reap the benefits, however, you must use morning saliva. Spit into your fingers and spread it on your face. It may sound untoward, but don't brush your teeth first. It will not work if your mouth is clean. Leave it on the face for about an hour then wash it off. Additionally, if you have warts, use the blade of a pair of scissors coated in saliva to make the wart go away. Open the scissors to its full capacity. Use the saliva and run the blade over the wart. This must be done every day. Do not lick the blades.*

If the women wanted plants, Grandmother parceled plants out stingily. She gave one of the women quick instructions on how to cook and drink the herbs. All the while, she yanked the plants roughly, bending the stems till they snapped and their scent filled the air with their pungent, acrid smells. Their fragrance covered her hands and their oils spread on her fingers, as she stuffed them into a reused plastic shopping bag.

For her family, she brought out the marijuana leaves steeped in cane alcohol. The marijuana leaves swam in the alcohol, having turned a pallid green. This concoction relieved muscle pain. The alcohol on its own was good for toothaches. Soaking a cotton ball and putting it on the pained tooth numbed the area for hours, until you could see a doctor or until you needed the next dose.

Doctors and dentists were a luxury. That meant paying for the bus and the appointment and the medicine. So, I sucked on that cotton ball in agony; knowing that

Grandmother's herbs were a staggering gift that I didn't want but desperately needed.

> *If your ears have been plugged up for a long while, it's time to use urine. This requires, of course, that you use someone else's pee. It won't work if you use your own. The urine must be warm and fresh from the bladder. Have the source fill a container. It is best to use a container that has a wide enough mouth to fit your ear into. Place the container over your ear and tip the other way. The urine should completely fill your ear and fix the problem. It's important to use caution with this remedy. You must create a seal or the urine will run onto your face and the cure will be spoiled. Also, do not kneel and have a parent urinate into your ear. This lacks dignity.*

Along with her herbs, she kept gallons of holy water in old milk cartons. From time to time, then obsessively, she'd sprinkle the water around to keep the demons at bay and purify her home. She imagined that every room was haunted. Those rooms felt haunted with a heaviness a specter couldn't possibly hold. But she went over the rooms, over and over again, thinking she could fix it with water a priest had said words over.

Those women didn't understand what my grandmother was taking from them. Exchanges with her were more than polite words and a few dollars; they felt thick like the liquids she warmed in her palm and injected into bodies.

Instead, the women became part of her imagination. They featured in her narratives as negligent mothers with too many boyfriends. They snuck around alleys and behind buildings to have sex and shoot drugs. In her mind, she twisted their bodies and dirtied their integrity. They were all as monstrous as she was.

When I was in the fourth grade, Grandmother walked me down the corridor of her house and towards the back door. She reached into an old vitrine and pulled out a syringe.

"Quiero que practiques en una almohada."

My eyes widened as she put the syringe in my palm. It was made of a thick, clouded glass. I tested the plunger to see how it felt. I imagined a human on the other end.

We walked to the front room, leading me into the dimly lighted living room.

"¿Quieres aprender o no?" she said to me.

"Sí. ¿Que hago?" I said.

We sat on the sofa in the living room, underneath her portrait. She leaned into me so closely that I could smell her perfume and dental cream. Huddled together, we looked like a family instead of a woman and child practicing to violate the law—hoping to violate bodies. She used a pillow to show me how to angle the needle and pierce the skin. She sent me home with the needle. My grandmother didn't have many syringes. I knew this was a precious gift. I wondered, as I walked home, whether I could do what she did. She was acting as a comfort to those women. She was a violator and a liar, but they didn't know that. Could I be like her?

I wanted her to love me. But I could feel how I was just another person thrown into her destructive storyline of women. In her mind, she was already weaving me into her perception of women as whores. I didn't want to be another red thread. Perhaps if she saw how special I was, she might love me more. In the environment of our home, I was already filling with frustration and sadness, and that was evolving into self-hatred. Could I be like Grandmother?

I walked into the house and into my room. I opened my dresser drawer and nestled the syringe amongst my underwear. In the next couple of days, I visited the syringe, wondering who I wanted to be. Wondering if I could ignorantly pierce another human with substances I didn't understand.

I took out the syringe and practiced on pillows, over and over. I waited to see if my grandmother would give me more instructions, more lessons. She didn't. But the sinister exchange stayed with me. Perhaps she'd been testing me. To see whether I was like her. To see if the rabid gleam of malice shone in my eye. To see if I was willing to make her some money or at least bring her some pride. But that wasn't who I was. What I remember is using the syringe to spray water on the bean plants I kept in my bedroom. And the awe I felt as I watched them grow out of their bags and tumble onto the floor.

# The Things in the Garage

FROM WHERE I STAND BY the door, I can see the sofa hanging upside down in the ceiling joists. The air smells of things pressed together too tight and forgotten. The sweat of the boxes rubs against the sweat of old books and the automotive tools. They are all together here, forced to live with one another even if they don't want to.

I don't know if it's secure, but it doesn't matter. Nothing about a garage has ever spelled safety for me.

The boxes are stacked almost to the ceiling but do not touch the sofa, which hangs from the middle of the ceiling. The garage is dim even in the light of the morning. That year, my grandmother has cats and kittens and as I stand in in the hazy darkness, I feel the fleas climb up my legs and begin to devour me.

I've always associated garages with animals. Grandmother's garage doesn't look like the one in our previous apartment, before we had to move in with her. That garage wasn't completely enclosed like this one. That garage was tight and completely open on one side. My dad drove into his spot. There was no door to protect the car. It's for this reason that one of the chickens had been able to build a nest and lay her eggs there. She was an angry chicken that tried to devour any person that ventured near. She fell into fits whenever we tried to get into the car.

I'm six years old when we move in with my grandmother. She gets me a dog. She says she loves animals. This thing is fluffy and small. Grandfather has built a doghouse that looks much like the chicken garage. Day in and day out, the fluffy dog stays in the doghouse. To ensure it stays there, my grandmother barricades the entrance. When I visit the dog, I press my fingers through the slats of wood that keep the dog in the dark. The dog licks my fingers.

My mom says that my grandmother loves animals. Perhaps it's me she hates. And that is why she hurts the dog.

My mom likes me nearby—within sight. I enter the garage to wash my underwear in the sink. My mother doesn't like me to put them in with the rest of the laundry. So, I pull out the wash board and scrub my underwear against the ripples of the board until my knuckles redden. The soap bites, but I scrub until I'm done and hang my intimates on the line.

When I'm eight, we move out of my grandmother's house. We move next door. That house doesn't have a garage.

When I'm in high school, my grandmother's garage becomes infested with rats. She stopped having cats a while ago. There was an incident with three cats she owned. She poured gasoline on them to get rid of the fleas; one of the cats suffered severe burns. My father was livid. I could hear him yelling from our house.

My mom sticks with her idea that my grandmother loves animals. But I can't help remembering over and over again, turning in my mind words my grandmother would say to me growing up. Whenever a cat or dog had a lot of fleas, Grandmother would lean towards me, "We should pour gasoline on it and light a match." She'd cackle at her own words. I would shrink away.

"She's joking," mom said to me.

"No," I said, "She's not."

"She's just messing with you."

"No. No. She means it."

"That's ridiculous. She loves animals, just like you do," she insisted.

In high school, I don't visit her much. By the time I'm in my teens, I know that she's mean. She has eleven grandchildren by then. Of her four granddaughters, I'm the eldest by a decade.

There is a rumor in the family that she only had four sons because she aborted every time she thought she was pregnant with a daughter. I don't know if it's true, but when she looks at me, my skin crawls. I have no doubt she was disappointed when I was born. I know, without a doubt, that she would have aborted me.

That Christmas, we all gather at her home. All her children and grandchildren show up to ply her with gifts. Her sons are desperate to please her.

Her youngest son gifts her an enormous Christmas tree. It's artificial like her old tree, but much bigger and much more realistic. My male cousins and I are at that age where we make fun of things. While the parents eat and talk to one another, we make fun of the Christmas tree in English.

"Grandma's tree looks like Christmas barfed on it."

"I think she put everything she could on it."

"Do you think there is a tree under there?"

Then someone says, "Did you see the elves?"

"Yea," I say, "those things are always creepy."

"No," my eldest cousin says, "look again."

My grandmother has had those same elves for as long as I can remember. They have plastic faces and fabric bodies. They smile—menacingly, I think. I get closer.

I don't squeal. Squealing would mean I'm frightened, and I've spent a good part of my childhood beating on these guys to get some respect.

The rats have eaten the plastic off the elves. Grandmother has chosen to display them as is. I can see the string of lights shining through the gaping holes in their faces. You can see the rats' teeth marks, where they gnawed the nose or checks off, as the elves smile back.

I'm out of college when my grandmother starts to use the garage as a residence. One of her sons leaves his previous family and starts up another. This isn't the first or second family this uncle has started. He is a serial family starter. Grandmother moves her son, his girlfriend and her son into the garage. They start to have more and more children.

I think about them in that garage. I wonder again and again whether the rats and fleas are still there.

At 24 years old, I pick up the phone to call Child Protective Services. Then hang up. Then pick up the phone again.

# Ethnography: Childhood Abuse and Why My Body Hurts

### *i.* *Introduction*

IN 2017, I'D BEEN WORKING at a local non-profit for almost five years when I suffered a major depressive episode. I've had depression since I was five years old. I remember playing on the swings at the back of my grandmother's house the first time I felt despair. My mom had told me a story of a people who beat themselves to stop sensation in their bodies. I slammed my wrist against the metal legs of the swing set till my skin was bright red. I wanted to stop feeling the intense pain I felt. I wanted to be numb.

At 44, I'd had the depression under control for over 15 years. I've experienced a lot of failures in learning to manage it. This time, I could feel the catatonia setting in. My speech was slowing down. I knew I needed intensive self-care, so I quit my job. During my job exit interview, the director said to me, "It makes sense that you are leaving. A certain percent of people leave when a director leaves." We had lost our old director eight months earlier. But he wasn't why I was leaving. In fact, I had shared my concerns with this director. She knew I'd been struggling with depression since October. She knew I loved this job. Consequently, her words hit me hard. For a second, I wasn't a person to her. I was a statistic.

The depression has an origin. I'm a survivor of sexual abuse. I come from a family of immigrants who came into the United States from Mexico. My grandmother had sons. Most, if not all, are pedophiles. The sons birthed mostly boys. I am the eldest girl by about 10 years—and one of the only two who actually grew up in this abuse. The other girl's mom got remarried and they moved away when my cousin was 4 years old. I lived alone in this—or so I thought.

This upbringing damaged my body.

## *ii.* Methodology

I've used a couple of studies to look at the effects of abuse on the body. The main study I used is the Adverse Childhood Experiences (ACE). The ACE study used a questionnaire to find out what types of abuse and neglect each participant endured as a child. They correlated this information with health measures and outcomes. The study was conducted from 1995 to 1997 by the Center for Disease Control (CDC) and Kaiser Permanente. It is one of the largest investigations of childhood abuse, neglect, later-life health and well-being.[1] Over 17,000 Health Maintenance Organization members from Southern California received physical exams and completed confidential surveys regarding their childhood experiences. These childhood experiences were compared with current health status and behaviors of the people involved in the study.

The ACE quiz measures different types of neglect and abuse people might have gone through as children. Initially, the test asked questions regarding: 1) physical neglect; 2) emotional neglect; 3) physical abuse; 4) verbal abuse; 5)

---

[1] https://www.cdc.gov/violenceprevention/acestudy/about.html

sexual abuse; 6) parental abandonment; 7) having a family member in jail; 8) having a mother who is a victim of domestic violence; 9) having a parent with mental illness; and 10) having a parent with a substance abuse problem. Eventually, these 10 items were put into three categories: abuse, neglect, and household dysfunction.[2]

What they found was that as a person's ACE score increases, so does the likelihood of the following health outcomes: alcoholism and alcohol abuse, chronic obstructive pulmonary disease, depression, fetal death, health-related reduced quality of life, illicit drug use, ischemic heart disease, liver disease, poor work performance, financial stress, risk for intimate partner violence, multiple sexual partners, sexually transmitted diseases, smoking, suicide attempts, unintended pregnancies, early initiation of smoking, early initiation of sexual activity, adolescent pregnancy, risk for sexual violence, and poor academic achievement.

Exposure to abuse, neglect, and household dysfunction leads to certain risk behaviors. It shapes who people are and how they navigate through the world. In particular, ACEs

---

[2] http://childrenshopeinitiative.com/resilient-youth-of-somerset-county/ace-study-and-findings

correlate with greater levels of "future violence victimization and perpetration" and have an impact on the "lifelong health and opportunity" of children. The more ACEs children experience, the higher their risk of facing medical, mental health, and social problems as they enter adulthood.

The findings of the ACE score are common sense. If you have a shitty foundation, you're going to have a hard time. But this study is unique in that there seemed to be a through line in how kids who had a bad childhood ended up with health problems. It was both revolutionary and validating for me to hear this.

I took the Adverse Childhood Experiences (ACE) survey in 2013, after attending a conference that talked about how childhood experiences affect health into the adult years.

My ACE score is high. I score a seven out of ten.

Abused kids often don't understand their own value and put themselves in situations that are dangerous and risky. We also develop behaviors meant to help us cope, like drinking or drugs. We try to numb ourselves. Because, we are stuck. Until we make the decision to choose to heal, we are trapped in the same nightmare. Even as time moves forward and things change, it replays in our minds. We relive the experiences that hurt us again and again and instead of making healthier choices that will help us heal, we continue to follow the same patterns, hoping to conquer what happened to us. But instead of moving forward, we pick at those scars like scabs, making them bleed, again and again.

While I feel like I could rant in long verses about the damage of my childhood, I think it's important to be transparent about what I have and don't have. I don't and never have abused alcohol. In fact, I've never had a hangover. I don't have Chronic Obstructive Pulmonary Disease (COPD). I haven't experienced a fetal death. I've never tried drugs. I don't have heart disease (ischemic or otherwise). I don't have liver disease. I didn't have an adolescent pregnancy.

But I do have depression. It's the clinical variety, which dramatically affects my motor skills. I've had financial stress most of my life. As I've gotten older, I realize I have issues with work performance. I've been married twice to very violent people. I've had more than one sex partner. But seriously, shouldn't everyone? I had an STD while pregnant with my son. His dad wasn't faithful. I've been a smoker. I've attempted suicide. I've had unintended pregnancies. I was at risk for sexual violence up until I was in my late twenties.

Another study by Jeanne McCauley, David Kern, and Ken Kolodner called "Clinical Characteristics of Women with a History of Childhood Abuse: Unhealed Wounds" found that there are other symptoms related to a history of childhood physical or sexual abuse in women. These include: "nightmares, back pain, frequent or severe headaches, pain in the pelvic, genital or private area, eating binges or self-induced vomiting, frequent tiredness, problems sleeping, abdominal or stomach pain, vaginal discharge, breast pain, choking sensation, loss of appetite, problems urinating, diarrhea, constipation, chest pain, face pain, frequent or serious bruises, and shortness of breath."[3] This study also found that women who were abused in childhood will continue to become victims of abuse as adults. [4]

---

[3] https://www.ncbi.nlm.nih.gov/pmc/articles/PMC1494926/

[4] https://www.ncbi.nlm.nih.gov/pmc/articles/PMC1494926/

Doctors call these somatization symptoms. They are symptoms that don't seem to have a discernable medical cause.

There's a combination of factors that turns abuse into poor health outcomes. Four basic aspects that are affected during abuse: the emotional, behavioral, social and cognitive pathways.[5] Together these affect adult health.[6] The emotional aspects affects mental health. The behavioral aspect includes health-related stuff like substance abuse, obesity, suicide, high risk sexual behavior and smoking. Social pathways include the ability to form and maintain social relationships. Quality of life is linked to positive quality social ties; without it, health suffers. Childhood abuse is also related to poor educational outcomes. Cognitive pathways include beliefs and attitudes; people will tend to have beliefs and perceptions that are unhealthy.

---

[5] Briere, J. Methodological issues in the study of sexual abuse effects. *Journal Consult Clinical Psychology.* 1992 Apr; 60(2):196-203.

[6] Kendall-Tackett, K. The health effects of childhood abuse: four pathways by which abuse can influence health. *Child Abuse Neglect.* 2002 Jun; 26(6-7):715-29.

I've had all of these symptoms, but my most frequent ones are nightmares, problems sleeping, back pain, frequent and severe headaches, pelvic pain, trouble breathing, and a choking sensation. I've had two uterine related surgeries; I grow things like cysts and fibroids. Recently, I started having urinary issues.

To say that abuse affects cognition doesn't begin to explain the large gaps in my memory. I'm stuck on certain events in my life. I almost can't remember any happy childhood memories. I'm not saying they didn't happen; I'm saying that I cannot access them. Events that were terrifying, vomit-inducing, and sad take up so much of my memory space that there isn't any left for happier memories. This issue with remembering things extends to all aspects of my life. I have to write things down to remember anything.

I numbed my feelings for many years. I wouldn't allow myself to process happiness or joy. I mainly felt anger and sadness. When I became an adult, it was very difficult for me to understand and name feelings like pleasure, elation, anxiety, satisfaction, pride, etc. I had to learn to re-label my feelings and accept all of them—and learn that they wouldn't crush me. I can't take compliments. Compliments are not part of my personal identity map.

I'm not always present in my body. In my youth, I could leave my body if things hurt or if I was frightened. As I've faced the abuse, I've lost this ability. I stay present in my body while at the dentist.

I'm uncomfortable with being seen or noticed. I like to stay in the background. I worked very hard to not be noticed in my family. It's a habit that is difficult to break.

I've had to learn new coping skills. I don't cut my skin when I'm devastated—even though I still think about it. Instead, I take deep breaths, I meditate. I label the emotion and feel the pain. I've learned how to talk to myself. "Everything is going to be okay. I know it feels awful right now. I'm so sorry for that. You don't deserve that. It'll be okay, honey. Hang in there. You've got this. This won't break you."

### *iii.* *Conclusion*

In my early thirties, I gave up the majority of my family. I couldn't forgive those that had abused me, and I couldn't forgive those that had looked away. I couldn't forgive their silence. Simply being with them made my entire body hurt.

As a kid, they ignored my pain. Instead, they protected the abusers because that benefited the entire group—the entire family system. I sincerely believe that they could not have done any different. They couldn't rebuild their own foundations, reject compliancy and submission, when it's what most of their relationships were made from. So, I let go. It was like cutting off a limb. I desperately miss those people I loved from the past, before I realized what their love meant. I won't be complicit to abuse. I can't pretend it didn't happen.

Abuse only happens in a system that accepts it.

I had a conversation with my aunt, Lupe, that changed the way I saw the household I grew up in. During a conversation she asked me why I hated her husband so much.

"He sexually molested me," I said.

"Oh," she responded, "You too, huh?"

I asked her to give me the names of the other girls involved. She named her sisters. I wasn't the first or the only one. To be frank, it took me a while to wrap my head around this. I was a number among many. The abuse hadn't started with me. This meant that I hadn't been the cause of it, as I had often suspected. I had always been told I was "bad." It hadn't occurred to me that it might not be true—that I wasn't the seed of perversion.

Ten years later, I was having a conversation with an activist friend. I told her about the abuse.

"Sexual abuse. It's taught. It's what happens when you can't say no to the smaller things," she said.

"What?"

"Think about it," she said, "Abusers can spot this. They want to see how far they can push something. It's why children need to be taught that saying "No" is okay."

"I knew that it was taught. My mom wanted me to be so compliant. I don't think she understood how much she was disarming me," I said.

I paused while I took control of the rage I was feeling.

I said, "I fought back."

"I didn't," she said.

One of the things that many dysfunctional families have in common is that they are built as a structure that supports abuse and abusers. People within that system, have decided the abuse is okay--or perhaps inevitable. They've gone through it and have decided that it "wasn't that bad" or that "I turned out fine." They pretend it isn't happening. They hide it, stuff it, silence it, and blame the victims.

I broke the chain of abuse with myself. I put myself in therapy—lots of therapy. I put myself in parenting classes. I broke apart from the system I grew up in and rejected their realities. I learned to say "No." I learned the value of children and women—and that eventually led to an examination of my own worth.

I envy my children and the life they get to have. I love that they get to be whoever they are without apology. I've taught them to speak up for their needs and self-advocate. But while these things bring me more peace, the abuse has left a large hole in my life.

I'm resourceful. I use whatever I have around me to build. I will call people, reach out. I'm an excellent problem-solver and am not limited by regular constructs of logic, or common sense, or certain patterns of behavior. I don't follow rules like that. I always think about all the rules I learned as a child, and how they didn't make sense. If those basics are moveable, anything else can move.

I'm resilient. I've failed countless times and understand that things don't stay that way. Even if the failure burns, I figure it out and stand back up. There just isn't anything worse than being abused as a child. There is nothing worse than having to see that person every weekend across the table for dinner, and remember the pain of when he penetrated you. Penetrated you with his betrayal and lies and fingers and objects. Nothing is worse than that. There is nothing worse than knowing you are alone, unprotected. There is nothing worse than understanding why my body hurts. My body might always hurt. And part of that pain is the fact that years ago, I cut off a limb when I gave up my family.

I will always be managing my depression. For me, The Adverse Childhood Experiences survey was a starting point— a flashlight at a time when I didn't fully understand how my childhood had crippled me. Those results don't change my body or the results of growing up the way I did. But it won't stay this way. Right now, I am doing what I've always done as a researcher. I'm gathering information. I'm trying to find avenues, loopholes, creative solutions that will point me in a direction that will fill me with peace, with calm, with grace.

I read a study recently that gave me hope. Researchers Laura A. King and Kathi N. Miner found that writing about trauma has perceived health benefits. I need to do more digging into this, but it looks promising. And unlike last time, I don't want to do this alone. I've spent so much time dismantling things and breaking away. I'd like this to be different. I'd like friends to come with me. Perhaps, we can build family around common passion—common ground. Perhaps we can heal together.

# Sick with Dog / God

*Third Grade*

MOM WAS SICK with god. Sitting there, on the steps of the school, she threaded her fingers through her thin hair searching for evil.

She had shoulder length, wavy hair that hid scars from a dog attack when she was four years old. The neighbor's dog had ravaged her head and developed a taste for blood.

I sat next to her, waiting for my third grade teacher to arrive.

Mom picked through her hair, feeling each strand.

"I found one," she said. She yanked quickly on the hair, as if it were fast and lithe with strength.

She piled it with the others on her thigh. She wore pants all the time. She was ashamed of her legs and didn't like to show them.

"How do you know which ones to pull out?" I asked.

"Well," she said, "You look for the bad ones."

I felt my own hair bound tightly into braids. She was fastidious about the appearance of my long hair. In the morning, she furiously brushed all the tangles out. Then she'd part my hair once and again and another time. I could feel the tip of the combs digging a line down my head. Having her brush my hair was an interesting compromise. For twenty or thirty minutes, I had her full attention. That attention came at a price. The entire time, she would pull and yank and criticize. That criticism was both for her and for me. But mostly, it was a measure of whether either of us were living up to her standards.

She wasn't just fastidious about hair. At night, she looked out the windows and checked the latches. At night, she rattled the doors to see if they were locked. Then, she checked the stove, touching all the knobs. She did this repeatedly, until whatever was inside her settled.

"How do you know which ones are the bad ones?" I said.

"They are thicker than your other hairs."

I thought deeply about her words. She was the wisest person I knew. She was thoughtful. She always tried to be kind. And she was gorgeous. Her skin was a pink porcelain. Her eyes were a greenish grey. And when she looked at me, when I thought she loved me, my entire being lit up.

We were alone on that campus. The occasional teacher went by and they nodded or waved. Before the first bell rang, she gathered her hair. It went round and round on her index finger till it was a tight wad.

I felt alone, sitting there with her. But I couldn't explain why. I thought her presence was supposed to make me feel full. She stood up—and she walked me to class.

She was very devout. Religion and insanity mixed in her head. Each hung on to the other as if they needed each other to stay afloat.

"Do you think I'm beautiful?" she asked me a few days later.

She thought it was so important to be beautiful. She dissected beauty in a way that was fascinating then and became revolting later.

"Yes, you are very beautiful. You are the most beautiful person in the world."

"What if I got fat? Would you still love me?" she said.

"Yes," I said.

I never asked her if she thought I was beautiful. I knew I didn't qualify. I wasn't even the right color.

"Liar," she said, "you wouldn't love me if I were fat."

"I'm not lying. Yes, I would. I would still love you," I said.

"What if I was obese?" she said.

"Yes," but I said it more tentatively. This was going somewhere bad and I wasn't sure I wanted to follow.

"See. I knew it," she said.

"I would still love you."

And I could have sworn that then. Her beauty filled my eyes. But she didn't feel the same way about me. Her eyes landed on me like nervous birds.

Her gaze felt hazy and gray.


*Fourth grade*

"I remember lying on the grass. It was one of those very hot days in Mexicali, where the air felt like you'd been shoved into an oven. My mother still owned the store, so I must have been around four. I was sick, so she'd taken me to the store with her. This was after the dog bit me. As I lay on the lawn, I could see that man who'd been stabbed. His intestines hung out. I

124

watched him stumble into the channel. Then I saw him tumble again and again. Over and over," she said.

"What happened to him?" I said.

"He'd been stabbed. I saw his intestines hanging out of his body. I heard his body had been found down in the channel."

"Did you see this happen?" I said.

"No, I just heard the adults talking about it."

But even then, I wondered if this is when her visions had started. Had god gifted her with seeing such horrible images? Or had seeing an eviscerated man tumbling down the canal, make her closer to god? Or perhaps the two things went together, like the saints she talked about.

Or possibly the spirits had entered her brain when the dogs split it open.


*Sixth grade*


125

"Am I the most beautiful person you know?" she said.

"No," I said.

"You used to think so," she said. She's downcast. This is the first time we've had this conversation in a while. I had been thinking carefully about what to say when she tested me again.

"I know that you are not the most beautiful, but I love you. I think that matters more," I said.

"You used to tell me differently," she said.

"I'm sorry. I know you aren't the most beautiful and I love you. That's important. I can see that you are not perfect and I love you *anyway.*"

Her silence told me she didn't think so.

"What matters is that you think I'm perfect," she said.

"What matters is that I love you," I said.

*High School*

"I think," she said, "those bugs are getting in the house because of you."

"Why do you say that?" I said.

"I think you are doing evil things. I think they are in the house because god is trying to scare you onto the right path. You need to pray more."

"I'm not doing anything wrong," I said.

She must have seen the fear in my eyes. Once she saw it, she came alive with it.

"You know I have prophetic dreams," she said.

"Yes, I know."

"I've seen what you do," she said.

I started meditating at age 16. It wasn't a serious practice yet. But it was the beginning of something. I would turn the lights off and light a candle, setting an intention.

"What is going on in your room?" she said.

"Nothing."

"If you weren't doing anything, you wouldn't need to close your bedroom door. You have to leave the door open a crack," she said.

"I'm just meditating."

"Candles remind me of Satan worshipping. And that music you play sounds Satanic and ritualistic," she said.

"It's not Satanic."

"It doesn't matter if I can't see what you are doing. God can see you. You are separating yourself from god. I don't like it. I can see you heading in the wrong path," she said.

But I wasn't listening anymore. I knew she didn't hear me. I saw her, but her gaze felt hazy grey.

*Now*

Sometimes, loss is endless. I learned about the long span of death when my mentor died some years ago. When people would ask me how he was doing I would say, "He's dying from cancer."

But months later, I was still saying the same. It was then that I better understood that loss is a life-long process. Sometimes loss is something that lasts for years, then decades. Just when loss has depleted the pit of the soul, it continues.

I was married for the third time when I went to her home and she had cardboard cut-outs of people on the windows. I looked at my husband with alarm. His eyes locked with mine.

"What's going on?" I asked her, once inside the house.

"What do you mean?" she asked.

"The cardboard people. What's going on?"

"Oh," she said, suddenly animated, "those took me such a long time to make."

"I can imagine."

"They are so people that are passing by think there are people in the house," she said.

"I think they will know they aren't real, Mom."

"No. They aren't going to figure that out," she said.

I could tell that she wasn't listening. She'd already decided what this meant. But she was excited and manically happy. I could see that her eyes had hazed over, and she had drifted away from reality.

I left a few minutes later. We never talked about the cut-outs again. I was training my gaze too. For me, it wasn't about blocking out the people who didn't fit my reality or expectations. On the way home, I closed my eyes to find that safe place inside of myself where I went to as a child when I realized Mom couldn't see me. In the car, I felt the relief of not having to live there anymore. I thought of the thousands of times I considered death to be a better form of freedom than the life I lived with her. I look at my husband, driving. He is kindness. He always sees me for who I am—not what he hopes I will be.

# Delusion

AT NIGHT, I GO INTO the backyard. I like being out there alone. The sounds of shrill, resentful voices from inside the house, as well as the loud clap of my loneliness, becomes a dull din when I'm alone in the dark.

I feel the cold air on the back of my neck and hair. I turn on the workshop lamp and take out my journal. This isn't a good time in my life. I'm twenty-three, and I can't wait to escape into my thirties and forties. I want to speed up time.

I've been in therapy for about two years. I'm aware that I have a lot of work ahead of me before I can begin feeling even slightly normal. Healing only happens with time.

On the other side of the wooden fence, I see a man leaning in to watch me. He reaches over the fence. He's a stocky, leather-faced immigrant, wearing a light brown shirt. His hand, as he grasps, is blunt and thick. He looks like my father's brothers. I turn quickly to get a better look, but he isn't there. He lives in the corner of my eye, as do all the rest of these men I see.

I'm 25 years of age. I'm walking down the hall of the school where I teach fifth grade. I feel the presence of another person coming towards me. Out of the corner of my eye I see a small statured man—hefty but diminutive—walk alongside in the opposite direction. He's wearing bleary toned pants—gray or brown—and a red shirt. I register the shapes and colors before he passes me and disappears out of the corner of my eye.

Sometimes I see people I know aren't there. This has been happening since I went into therapy four years ago and I unhooked the memories from their anchors.

Memories float. No matter what you do, whoever you were 15 years ago can float to the surface to haunt you. It doesn't matter if you are ready or if you are walking back to your classroom.

I take a deep breath and decide to ignore the man I just saw. I'm shaken. I take a deep breath and tell myself it is okay. It's not, of course. But I'm very good at rearranging realities to match my needs. It's a trick I learned from my tumultuous childhood.

At this school, I am working with the children from my neighborhood and it's breaking me. I see children going through the same abuses I did. This time, it's my responsibility to protect them and this terrifies me as much now as it did when I was a child.

I'm not delusional. I go through an exacting process.

Do I like what I see/feel/know?

*No.*

Is there anything I can do about it?

*No.*

Okay, let's change our attitude to cope.

*Okay, but this doesn't feel good.*

Noted.

I don't talk to my psychiatrist about the people I see. I know she'll heavily medicate me. I strongly suspect this is posttraumatic stress disorder. The problem with PTSD is that it prefers to unsettle you just as you feel you are moving beyond those memories. When you feel strong, the memories appear, waiting for resolution.

Instead, I go to my therapist. The words spill out of my mouth with trepidation.

"Is it men?" she asks.

"Yes. How did you know?" I say.

"It's out of the corner of your eye?" she says.

"Yes."

"Do they look like the men who hurt you?"

"Yes," I say.

"That's common with people who have had sexual abuse. I'm sorry," she says.

"I'm not crazy?"

"No," she says, "You are just healing."

"Healing feels awful. Why am I doing this to myself? I just want it to stop."

"Because," she says, "you want something better for your children."

"Yes. Yes, I do."

But for a moment, I think about quitting. Why do they call it healing when it feels like being ripped open?


I don't look it up. The internet was newer and didn't have the breadth of information it contains now.

At that time, I was not an adept computer user. I wouldn't have known what to look for. Do I google "symptoms of abuse" or "visions out of peripheral vision"? Or do I just lay in emotional nudity, "Why do I see men who look like the men who abused me? Wasn't the experience enough?"

Typing up that search on a computer would have been more than I could manage. Writing things brings a new level of reality. It's no longer in your head. You've let out the thoughts to make words and that beast uncurls and begins to evolve. It becomes harder to pretend you don't see it—that it doesn't exist.

Writing makes things real. I like where things are. I prefer those images curled up in a tight ball inside my head, floating like all my other thoughts—bits of lint and fluff drifting in a vast tangle of deeper thoughts, beliefs, and memories.

Thoughts and memories of fear, floating amongst the clumsy words of kindness I use to talk to myself.

I'm 26. I'm at my mom's house in the bedroom that used to be mine. I'm changing clothes after a workout. I reach back to unlatch my bra. As I slide down the straps, I turn my body slightly. I see someone outside my window looking in on me. It's broad daylight. I'm furious.

I put on a T-shirt and walk into the living room to make a head count. Everyone who is supposed to be there is there. But people walk in and out of my mom's house like it's a train station. They stop to chat, or rest, or use the bathroom.

I look at their faces. They seem calm.

"What's going on? Why are you making that face?" Dad says.

"It's fine," I say, "was anyone in the backyard just now?"

"Why?" he says, "What happened?"

"Nothing. Nothing."

The shame of being watched silences me; shame always silences me. I don't need the men in my family to maintain a tally of how many men have seen me naked. I don't need them to talk amongst themselves about which of them have seen me naked. I don't want them to talk about me. I don't want to be a word bandied in their mouths.

There are multiple entrances into the backyard and I know I heard the clang of the kitchen door. Whomever that was knows I saw them.

I've never felt safe in my mom's house.

My aunt committed suicide when I was 25 years old. Her conspiracy theories turned out to be a bit more than we expected. She left a single note to her eldest son:

"Jose, take care of my mother."

She's dead inside her one-bedroom apartment till her sister finds her. All the signs were there. She was a prescription drug addict. She was heavily medicating in order to sleep and make it from one day to the next. She was telling us stories that didn't make sense. She was missing work and her friends had started to call me to tell me they were worried about her.

In her car, she heard voices. She turned up the car radio so loud, I couldn't hear my own thoughts. And she couldn't hear the voices.

She was locked inside her own head, adrift in schizophrenia before anyone even thought to look for her. She must have been unbearably alone, living in this world while the rest of us lived in ours.

But I don't have schizophrenia. When I gather the courage to speak to my psychiatrist, she tells me I'm fine.

"How do you know that?" I say.

"Because you are asking me. People that have schizophrenia don't ask. They don't ever doubt what they are seeing," she says.

Her office is filled with stuffed animals and incense and Buddhas. I look down at her thumb. She chews on it when she's nervous. Today, she's wrapped a band aid around it to prevent the chewing. Does she know what I'm going through?

I want to pass over this phase of my healing instead of through it. I rage every time I'm at her office. I'm angry. I tell her it's unfair.

That dull doubt is my saving grace. I know my tía never doubted the voices she heard. They were part of her reality. No second thought. My wondering is that fine line between us— her and me.

While the doubt fills me with uncertainty, I'm grateful for it.

The flashbacks continue for about five more years. Those years feel like decades. Then the healing process shifts and instead of experiencing images as part of the PTSD, it becomes a lot scarier. I'm in a safe place. I'm happily married. I'm far from my family. Most of them don't know where I live. Instead, those relatives become foggy memories in my mind. Once the flashbacks ease up, I begin to remember happier things. I remember gathering around my mom's kitchen table, talking with the other women. When I remember this, I don't remember their death pacts or their depression; instead I remember the comfort and warmth of their presence—the predicable affection that surrounded me.

At the same time this is happening, my brain has decided it's time for the next phase of healing. I stop seeing flashbacks in the form of images. Suddenly, I'm hit with the emotions. I feel someone hovering over my bed and pressing me down, and I'm terrified.

"I'm so frightened," I tell my husband. "Please hold me and tell me that everything is going to be okay."

"What's scaring you?" he says.

"I don't know," I say, "please hold me."

But I do know. The memory is non-specific and barely an image. It's more like a sensation. But I know where it comes from. I'm a child and I'm being stalked. I'm afraid and terrified. I feel like a small animal, and I know he's going to get me. He will devour me, and I will be gone. Erased.

One time too many as a child, I had to pretend I wasn't scared, wasn't anxious, wasn't angry. I denied all the emotions. And now, all those feelings are crawling back expecting to be seen, to be noticed, to be called by name. They want to come out of hiding.

In the warmth of my husband's arms, I talk to myself.

"You are safe. Everything is okay," I tell myself.

I've gotten better at speaking to myself with kindness. When my emotions are settled, I pick them apart slowly. I honor them for what they are and hope that they forgive me.

"That is fear," I say.

"That is anxiety. This emotion is temporary. I can feel it without being swallowed. I'm okay."

"That is loathing. But I don't need to hate myself. I did the best I could with what I had. I had good instincts and here I am on the other side. It's okay," I tell myself, "I am safe and no one is going to hurt me. I have many more resources now. I know how to take care of myself."

I soothe the feelings till they are quiet. I rock them to sleep like babies. Feelings don't have any logic. They are there to be accepted. Just like children. When my own children are not okay, I hold them and love them and reassure them. Here I am doing the same for myself—and hoping I can teach myself how to love myself better.

I compel the hidden men at the corner of my eye to never return. I stare at my life straight on.

# Sewing Machine

MOM'S SEWING MACHINE FACED THE window to the backyard. She needed natural light to help her see. She also used the light that shone from the footer of the machine, and an industrial work light attached to the one corner, that came standard with all industrial machines.

The machine was a massive rattling monster that my mother borrowed from her mother-in-law. Mom earned three cents a collar to sew crocheted necklines on mass produced muumuus of wrinkled gauze. She'd taken on this work to contribute to the household within the limitations my father had set.

Sitting there, passing the fabric beneath the footer of the machine, she worked from home in silence, while I squeezed beneath her chair and played with the fuchsia threads that rained onto the floor.

The woman she worked for gave her three huge trash bags filled with precut fabric pieces and a large spool of thread. The boss lady was a thickset, shifty woman who paid her workers half a penny per piecework.

Mom sat on the kitchen chair curved over the machine. The noise was deafening. The machine moaned and hummed while mom lined up the fabric, guiding the pieces under the footer. She bent low. She made the same motions again and again as her hands turned into claws and her eyes dimmed.

That day, the fabric was bright pink. The next day's material would be black or dark blue.

Black, blue, fuchsia.

In her lungs, the beautiful colored threads formed a tapestry. Inside her, these shaped an abstract landscape meant to invoke emotion rather than show a static visual arrested in time. The threads changed with her breath. They shifted and moved like a living organism slowly inching its host towards death.

The fabric slowly killed her.

The chest ached. The lungs stopped working competently. Did the dust take up the space needed for oxygen? Or did it crowd the lungs to make them ineffective? Perhaps the lungs, upset at the foreign matter ceased—struck against unjust work and unfair practices. And refused to continue working. They called it chronic pulmonary disease. But it was much greater still—it was lungs unwilling to work under unreasonable circumstances.

Mom ripped the seams to re-sew and start the piece again. In the powdered sun streaming though the blinds, I saw dust particles flying all around. As she ripped the seams, red fuchsia lint fired into the air. I saw the lint playing with the dust, round and round. Mom coughed and her spit swirled the dust to merriment. She breathed in and coughed again.

Twenty years later, I work from an old, torn, leather chair in a building with so many floors, I feel as small as those people I can see from the windows. The many windows provide brightness, but the materials I'm working with are so dark, I can't see the light.

I'm officially a coder for the research department but I'm more than that. I'm a weaver. I find all the strands in the narrative of the interviews. I find all the colors that go together. I knit them together. Then check to see what other colors are contributing to the whole picture. Most of the time, I have no idea what I'm making.

I use software to pull apart meaning from the interviews I have uploaded to code. The interviews are part of a study on racism and bigotry within this school district. I'm not usually a member of this team; I've been borrowed from another team to help rescue the information they collected. This is a five-year project but no one took the time to look at whether the data being collected ever made sense.

I am grateful that the interviewed teachers are honest. But their responses scare me. If this is what they felt comfortable saying aloud, I can't imagine what they kept quiet.

"Everyone knows that you're supposed to punish black children harder than other kids. They don't get any discipline at home," says another teacher.

"Hispanic kids don't listen. They aren't taught to listen. Their parents are always working and let them run wild."

"Black girls are so loud and dramatic."

I put these responses in categories: Unequal punishment; negative perception. I tried to see this for what it is: data.

I learned how to code data in a college class. The professor brought in toys made of metal and wood and plastic. The elephants and dogs mixed with rhinos, cars and balls. I worked silently, sliding the animals back and forth, trying to figure out how they came together best.

But these aren't animals. These are children and the implication of the teachers' words make me wonder how they run their classrooms. I have no doubt the students can feel the hate directed at them.

In the interview responses, I look for patterns that might help me understand what is happening. Like my mother, I count on patterns to guide me. I count on the wisdom of their tempo. Patterns have their own tone and rhythm like threads that must be separated then brought together to make a picture. Right now, those threads are tangled in my fingers and the effort to hold them makes my limbs ache. I hurt for these children.

My mom used patterns in the same way. But instead of ending up with an image that would be described in a report, she ended up with pants or a dress.

I crank out those bits and pieces, letting the information tell me how it plans to become a whole. Like my mother, I'm trying to piece something together. Like her, I cut out the bits that don't help or don't belong.

Standards for the workplace don't exist when you work from home and get paid in cash. The avocado green vinyl kitchen chair was worn down through the cotton and exposed the wood seat. Mom didn't have an ass. She sat there grinding her bones into wood. Her entire body shook with the rattling machine. She couldn't control the cotton dust threads that clung to her clothes. Bright pink dust grabbed at her skin like glitter.

But she was no dancer. She was no whore. Or was she?

She ripped the seams apart.

"This isn't good," she mumbled.

She sewed. She reworked a piece worth three cents for 30 minutes if she had to. She believed in perfection, even under severe circumstances. She was stuck. This might break her, but at least she knew who she was.

This job isn't what I thought I would be doing. I studied to be a teacher, but I quickly learned that I wasn't built for that job. I worked at a school with high child abuse and special needs rates. My classroom was filled with children from severe to moderate poverty. Many came from abusive households. In my classroom, I had a student who got locked in dark closets by his mom. I also had a child who'd been beaten with a wire hanger. Another girl would handle classroom disappointments by stapling her skin. She was a self-flagellator, who had constant bladder infections and chronic headaches.

I was trying to teach math and writing, while many of my students were in survival mode, trying to get through the day. They were trying to get enough food and avoid punishment. There was hardly any room for them to learn or thrive.

I taught fifth grade and I knew that many other teachers had seen the same things I was seeing, but had decided not to do anything. The last year I taught, I had a student in my classroom who liked to kill and torture animals.

Trying to help any of them meant arguing with the office for resources—every single time.

My teaching career didn't work out. I know that my mom's aspirations were to stay at home, but that didn't work out. She took a job. I had to take a job. There wasn't much difference between our choices. Her work was killing her and mine was killing me. Except I think she knew the work was wearing her down. I had no idea that these words were diminishing me. I had no idea that the inequities I was working with were taking bite sized pieces of flesh with them. I got smaller and smaller.

At night, her back hurt. I could hear her moan and cry out as my father massaged her shoulders. In a few minutes, she got up to get a painkiller.

I capture each teacher's words. I create themes and write conclusions. I stitch it all together into a report backed with anecdotes, numbers, and facts. I swallow the hate until it becomes a headache. At night, I take a painkiller and go to bed.

When I finally write it down, I know how to prove what I am saying. I pull quotes and examples. But I have no idea what it really means. At the time, I thought it meant that this was unfair and that I was angry and stressed and anxious.

When I finish the report, it is still this abstract thing that I barely understand. I write for a man who has a doctorate and is clearly taking advantage of me. Every time I finish part of my work, he gives me more of his.

At the time, I am too green to consider how I am adding to the inequity. I turn in reports, but it isn't enough. Teaching hadn't been enough and this wasn't enough. This isn't even a gauzy muumuu with a crocheted neckline. At least a muumuu has substance. It lives in its own space, clearly defined as something to wear when you don't want too much fabric to pet your skin. But this? My own work? I don't know what this is. All I know is that I can't touch it.

Like those children, I am a minority that came from poverty. I'd suffered the same bigotry. I know how often my teachers told my mom that they loved having me in class because I was "quiet and never said a word." They were right. I was quiet. I had mostly white teachers. I can't imagine that they ever cared about what I had to say or what I felt.

I'm paid by piecework like my mother. And I'm no more important. No more unimportant. I like to think that what I'm building is more than a muumuu, but I haven't seen evidence of that. Like her, I am a woman trying to piece things together into a whole that makes the world make more sense for me and maybe for others. For me, it is those beliefs, those morals, those practices that come alive in a report that I think might make things better. But is it? How much is effort worth? Perhaps thirty cents apiece—and only if it's perfect?

For my mom, those pieces came together—and became money. But we were both counting on the same thing. We both hoped that our work might improve things, and we both hoped that our work didn't compromise who we were.

The truth is, I wove awful pieces while I worked there. I was unpracticed. I was young. I didn't know where I was headed yet. I saw that the world was moving too slowly for progress in women's rights, in children's rights, in lesbian, gay, bisexual, transgender, queer (LGBTQ) rights. The world wasn't fair for African-Americans and Latinos. Most people still didn't understand about humility and standing back to learn from each other. The world wasn't changing as fast as I needed it to be. I was still that poor brown girl with the mom who had sewed, earning money outside the American system.

But while Mom worked isolated in her room, bent low, focusing on only the stitches that shaped her piece, I began to look up higher and search for other women willing to work with me. I looked for more than progress. I wanted to be less alone. I wanted connection. I wanted others who saw the inequity with me and were willing to riot. But I didn't know that yet. It would be at least 10 years before I saw my weaving as a collective art process.

In that office with the windows, I took a color around each knuckle and wove the threads. Honesty is important. I threaded those images, dark or dank or hopeful or emerging. I worked until my fingers hurt, not knowing that I was silently ingesting the fibers into my body when I got too close, and that I would eventually need to save myself from drowning in the injustices that I saw all around me—and that I was unwilling to accept and swallow down.

# Vestiges of Courage

I KNOW COURAGE. I'VE FELT it like a sharp yank in the right direction. Even when I've been afraid, it pulls on me at the edges of my consciousness. It's that sensation that can only be verbalized with the words "Fuck it. I can't live with the consequences if I do it any other way."

My courage is directly connected to my morality and ethics. For me, more than anything else, action is the logical result of doing the right thing and knowing what I can live with. The other things don't matter to me. I don't always think about my own safety. I don't do what is easy or convenient. I don't give up even if the rest of the group doesn't agree with me. I don't mind standing alone. I don't care if that means I am hated. I don't care if the group ostracizes me and I'm alone.

And I won't be silenced because it shames.

It's painful. Courage hurts. Courage can burn as hotly as the hells my mom told me about.

My mom, like me, was a storyteller. She retold me stories she had heard on the radio as a child, or stories her parents had told her. At night, she read from the Goldenrod Bible while we sat around her. She retold me novelas that she had watched years past. She recounted songs as stories.

She told me stories whether or not she remembered the entire thing. So, her stories sometimes had holes like mysteries my own mind craved to fill in. I am a storyteller because she built me this way.

In Mexico, we sat around as my grandfather—her dad—sang us songs. In that day underneath the blazing yellow of heat, as we tore open the skin of the pomegranates, he told us this story about Satan and a bet he had going with a mortal man. This story was old. The origins were not Christian. I was 15 years old, but as he told it, I could feel the weighted edges of a story that had been formed many years past. But here, in this instance, it felt like air. The story had been handed down over decades. And it felt worn like parchment softened with wear. With wear, threadbare and thin, but still alive.

"Lucifer was at the festivities of the…." he told, "Juan Diego challenged him to eat a pomegranate without dropping a single seed…"

He laughs at his own story.

"Can you imagine that? Juan Diego was a man of God. The devil thought he could beat him. So, Lucifer said, 'Yes'. Lucifer was vain and thought he could do anything. But he couldn't. He split open that pomegranate and the seeds spilled out."

He laughs again. He delights in the triumphs of this mortal who foiled Satan. He sits silently watching us split our pomegranates open. I finger the seeds as they drop, spattering on the ground, leaving their imprint on the cement.

I'm not small for a woman. I'm 5-foot, 4 inches and border on the edges of being "too hefty for a woman of my height." But at 13, I was slightly built. At that time, the cholos in our area were training their dogs to fight. I'd see the gangsters strutting in front of our home, their strides a practiced feigned relaxation, slow and lazy with hips jutting. They walked their bulldogs in the heaviest of chains. Their dogs, pulled violently and angrily.

In this neighborhood, people kept their dogs chained. There were no yards to speak of and it was uncommon for people to keep their animals indoors. So, once free of the 3-foot space they inhabited on a daily basis, these dogs unleashed their raging power.

I was in our yard that day. When I saw two cholos with dogs, I became frightened. The dogs pulled and snapped at one another. It was common knowledge that they trained their dogs to fight. These dogs weren't raised as pets. They were raised as weapons.

I imagined a blood bath. I imagined dogs yelping in pain, confused about why they were being hurt. I imagined puppies. Puppies that hadn't gone to a good home.

I turned behind me, grabbed the hose and turned it on. When I saw the cholos positioning their dogs to fight, I aimed the hose at them. They looked up at me. At first, they seemed stunned. Once they identified me, they yelled.

"Hey!"

But I ignored them and continued hosing. The water arched strongly beyond our fence, beyond our sidewalk and into the street. I didn't stop until they dispersed. I never made eye contact.

I practice where to stand. That's what life feels like to me—a figuring out of where I stand. It is a practice in dignity. It is a practice in understanding how I might have changed. It is a practice of self-realization and how I hold my truth outside my body.

From the moment I can remember till the time I was 16 years old, every weekend, I had lunch or dinner across the table from the man who molested me. My parents hosted him and his family. They encouraged me to be polite. My mom knew early on what had happened. That same person had a feast with the girls in our family—going from one girl to the next until we were all irrevocably damaged and broken. All of us became self-flagellators. Stunned and confused by the "absence" of ongoing abuse, we continued it on our own.

In Spanish, courage translates to a word closer to valiant—this word is "valor". But there is another word that can also mean courage—and is closer to rage. This word is "coraje". This word describes my defiance better than anything. My courage is flavored with rage and a need to reject conformity. During those weekends, I escaped, when I played with the boys or I played in my room. When I got older, I stopped trying to engage anyone. I was 15 years old and unwilling to fulfill the role I'd been assigned.

Both parents saw this as a defiance, as disobedience, a falling out with the practices they had instilled in me about humility and my role of servitude as a woman.

Both these things were starkly true. But there are some other truths there, too. My mom accepted this dangerous man being around me. I've been looking for what caused this ongoing act by her. What made this okay, acceptable? A hallowed tradition that wouldn't be broken?

She must have done what she thought was right. But guided by what? Like Juan Diego, she faced the devil. Like the devil, he was vain and confident.

But I am much more than a story.

I see her hoping that her faith in god might help me. Like Juan Diego, she wanted to face the evil and come out unscathed. There is a deep part of me—that part that was her child then—that needs to think that she was courageous.

I want to imagine her draped in the mail of goodness, of god, coming onto Lucifer and defeating him due to her character. But this isn't true, of course. This thing that I want to be believe is a lie. There was no courage there. There was fear and a need to conform and keep the peace. She was limp with indecision. She prayed because she couldn't do anything else.

When I was 21 and divorced, I saw her more clearly. I had a restraining order on my ex-husband. We had an agreed-on child visitation schedule, and I expected him to follow it—to conform to the laws of the country he lived in.

Because I wouldn't speak to him, he called my mom. She spent hours on the phone talking to him. Sadly, if you add up the hours they spoke to each other in my twenties, it would never add up to the amount of time she and I spoke to each other at that time.

"Stop talking to him," I begged.

"I can't," she said.

"Why do you do that? Why do you always betray me?"

"You are being very stupid," she said. "You can manipulate this man. He loves you. He's crazy about you. You aren't playing this right."

"I don't want to be around him, Mom."

"You need to be strategic."

"No. You need to stop," I said.

"You don't understand what I am trying to do. I am doing this for you."

"No," I said, "you're not. Stop telling him where I am."

"I can't lie!"

"Stop talking to him," I said.

"I can't do that. You don't get it! I *wish* someone loved me like he loves you."

I wish I could say that this was an isolated moment in our lives. But it isn't. I can still see her there, facing and trying to defeat this evil. But every time she told him where to find me, and he would appear at my school or at the store to watch me, I stopped believing in her a bit more.

We had this same conversation twenty times—until our relationship deteriorated, and I couldn't look at her anymore.

In the face of adversity, I wondered if she followed her heart. I wondered whether this was a kind of courage I didn't understand.

When I was deeper into my twenties, I saw her in the car with the man who molested me. She spent hours in that car talking to him. He was desperate because his wife—my mom's niece—was pushing him out of her life. The woman who had told me not to be alone in a car with a man, was in the car with the man I most hated.

The woman who had taught me compassion was taking it too far. She stretched that compassion beyond the limits of my understanding. As I saw her in that car, I wondered at her valor, or at her betrayal of our beliefs or her need to conserve the family. I wondered and wondered until these things didn't mean what she told me they had. And I had to redefine everything.

A few months after that meeting in the car, her niece came to me. We went to court together and I helped her get a restraining order. I can't call this courage. I need to call it what it is, love and rage.

I sat with her as she told me her story in Spanish and I translated it into English on the court document. I wrote it all out as she watched me and told me what to add and edit and delete. She spoke English but she stumbled over it.

I wrote down every detail firmly, unafraid of the truth, knowing that silence is deadly.

"Don't write down that he raped me," she said.

"You have bruises on your arms. I'm having the police photograph those."

"No," she said.

But I continued to write, undaunted.

I know now something I didn't know then. That anyone who is abused, or raped, or hit, or devoured by another person, has the right to re-enter the world in whatever way they need to. They can enter it limping or dragging. They have a right to show up bruised or unfailingly whole—appearing as if nothing happened—and pretending their life shines like a gift of great fortune. It's not my place to judge.

In the end, my mother's niece and I compromised on what was in that document. I let go and she let go.

"Do you want to prove that you deserve this restraining order or not?"

"Yes," she said.

"You need to understand something," I told her, this woman who had helped to shape me. "This restraining order is only as strong as you are. If you don't do what's needed to uphold it, then we are both wasting our time."

"I can do this," she said.

She didn't. But her journey wasn't my journey. I seethed at what I thought was her failing. Now, I understand that she was putting one foot in front of the other as carefully as she could, while she navigated her new understanding of herself and the voices in her head that interrupted her thoughts.

But I knew that her sons knew she was getting raped. I knew they could hear her getting hurt. I knew they heard her calling for help. And I knew they were silent.

I broke my silence after her death. I was twenty-seven when I decided to call social services. It is true what my mom always said about me. I am direct and rude. I am callous. I am unwilling to think about what is good for everyone. I can be, like she said, pedantic and unemotional. She's right when she said that I was willing to run over everyone to get what I want. She was right and I am not sorry.

The man who had molested me had children living in his house—including a young girl I loved. I couldn't live with a decision of inaction. I couldn't guiltlessly navigate the world without doing anything.

On the day that social services visited their home and told them the children couldn't live there, their mother called me.

There was no preamble.

"Did you call social services?" she asked.

"Yes," I said. I wanted to defend myself and my life. I wanted to talk about the pain and the shame and the humiliation I wanted her daughter to avoid. I wanted to tell her how much I loved her little girl. I wanted to say that the shame is stifling and choking and that she might feel like drowning for the rest of her life. I wanted to tell her that this family lied and stuck together. But I didn't say those things.

"I'm sorry if I hurt anyone," I said.

"I called to thank you," she said.

I don't remember the rest of that call. I might have cried with relief. I might have raged. I might have spilled truths.

But I don't remember. And it doesn't matter. I felt the pull of what was right and what felt like love and I didn't question it. It's likely that everyone in that family found out what I did. They already hated me, and I can't imagine this made them love me more.

By that time, I had lost everyone in that family who I loved. I couldn't look at my mother or father and my brother was gone. I couldn't face Mom's family. My grandmother was dead and my mom's niece had killed herself.

My father's family was monstrous. Their opinions, their beliefs, those things that made them hide in the shadows while they committed their depraved acts on children, those people don't matter to me. They can burn.

And I am not the Juan Diego of my grandfather's story. I am not clever. I don't have faith. In fact, I have rejected religion and all that it stands for. Instead, I am simply a woman—a mother. I know what I'm made of. I am made with an angry love that rages hot. I am made with an angry valor that will burn me and the whole family down.

I may have been born from that family. I may have been born from my mother and made by my father. I was carved from that family and damaged as I went from hand to hand. But I was never the girl they wanted to make me into. Instead, I am a woman who carves thumbs into the pomegranate that is my family. I watch as the juices stain my fingers and delight as the seeds tumble to the ground, leaving their red marks all over the ground and onto my clothes.

# The Bridge

I HEARD SPANISH FIRST.

I slipped into the world deafened by my mother's cries. Her songs were familiar. Her voice was familiar. But her anguish was primordial.

Her anguish didn't need to be broken into meaning. It lived in the cells of my body and shaped my muscles.

The nurses pumped my nose and cleared my mouth till I could breathe enough to wail. They cooed in their unfamiliar words. They spoke to me—but what were they saying?

I only understood English much later. Until I understood linguistic isolation, I couldn't wrap my head around this break. Why wasn't I learning English? My family existed kilometers of understanding away from other families in America.

We were geographically present but culturally remote. For all our efforts to have green cards, legal jobs, and be law-abiding, we still didn't fit in.

I picture my aunt, Belia, at the hospital. She doesn't speak English. Her 13-year-old daughter is translating. The doctor needs to tell my aunt that her other daughter is dead.

The doctor is too tired or too stupid or too lazy to get a professional translator. So, the thirteen-year-old does it instead.

But she doesn't know what terminology to use to get her mother from devastation to understanding.

And she knows.

She knows that the news will create a chasm in her mother. All she can do is say the words correctly from English to Spanish and hope that the words don't break her.

My 13-year- old cousin is so scarred by the memory that she clenches her jaw as she tells me this story. She wants to talk about unfairness and not dissolve into the pain of that experience. For her, that memory is a wound that doesn't scab over. All she can do is blur that memory with medication, or alcohol, or pretend it didn't happen.

My aunt never understood why her daughter died. That's what linguistic isolation is like. It's a sharp bite in the dark. It's a sharp bite by an animal you can't name.

What happens when families don't understand? When they can't integrate? When they can't intellectualize the world around them? When they don't know the rules of how to fit in? They create myths. They create a collective understanding of the world. *We* create a collective understanding of the world. We become isolated.

I become the bridge between my family and America. I was born here. I'm supposed to be integrated. But I feel my brown skin like a dirty mark that sets me apart.

I don't want to be a bridge. I don't want that job. At 10, I don't want to know that much about life. I don't like calling the telephone company to find out whether they've received the payment Mom sent. I don't like making decisions about critical documents. I don't like translating to teachers as my mother asks embarrassing questions.

I'm too honest to lie.

"Mrs. Bradford," I say, "My mom wants to know if I'm good. She wants to know if I behave good or bad."

I already know the answers, but I go through the dance anyway. This feels too intimate. Too much like I'm invading my own privacy.

I'm the bridge.

People believe it's great to speak another language. But I'm stuck in an in-between place, with one foot on either side. I'm not quite a native Spanish speaker. I'm not quite a native English speaker. Instead, I speak English with a thick accent that I hide. I speak Spanish in an accent I can't hide. I stumble through Spanish like I'm Velcro on Lycra.

I stutter. I stutter in Spanish. It's like a performance. I'm bare. Consciously aware that I'm not an equal. When I open my mouth and the words begin to crank out, then stop, then crank.

Am I a fraud? Am I not Mexican enough? Am I too American? I'm too dark skinned to be an American.

When I speak Spanish, I hear, "You're not white enough to be talking like that. ¿Tan prieta. Quien te crees?"

In English, I hear, "You're pretty smart for a Mexican. Your English is pretty good."

I take comfort in English. It's the language of my intellectual development. I learn poetry and literature in this language.

I develop a passion for Emily Dickinson in high school. I savor her dark tones around my tongue. My Spanish mouth can taste the humid dank of her words.

I want to be alone like her. I want to be trapped in a room where I write on bits of scraps. Instead, I'm in a home constantly filled with people who like to talk. Pencils and pens are constantly misplaced. My mom's home is always open to family. The house is filled with laughter and gossip and chaos. I'm trapped amongst the group.

I feel Dickinson's isolation deep like my own. I long for death with her as her fly buzzes. But I'm here, instead.

Spanish is the language of god. I learned religion in Spanish. I took Catechism with twelve other children from a neighboring lady who lives on our street. We sat on the floor in her roach-filled living room, in the stifling heat while the fan blew at our primers made from cheap newsprint.

From the time I was born to the time I prayed in Spanish every night, my mom, a dedicated Catholic, read to us from a yellow Bible she'd gotten from the Jehovah's Witnesses.

Alone in her room, mom read the New Testament to herself. As soon as she finished, she started again.

Later, as I learned the Bible in English, I had to translate it into Spanish before I understood it. At that time, my god spoke Spanish. And because he spoke Spanish, everything he had created was in Spanish.

Miracles were in Spanish. Spirituality was in Spanish. The meaning of life was in Spanish.

My mind is split into languages. Now, who's the bridge? How do I bridge myself into a whole?

# Voiceless

I WORKED IN A FACILITY for severely developmentally disabled children before I had my son Nathan. "Disabled" is what we called children who were different at the time.

As a culture, we hadn't considered that these kids—who were often dumped into this facility—were something other than what they had been labeled. They were the disabled. We were the abled. We never considered that they might have something to teach us.

The idea that they might present a dramatic interpretation of the standard never occurred to us. We never considered that we might need to rethink what it meant to be a person.

Communication comes in many forms. It's not always through verbalization. I learned that screaming is communication. Laughing is communication. Not eating is communication. But most importantly, children throwing shit was communication. This last one disturbed me.

"Don't react," staff said to us during training, "the children need to learn that they can't get a reaction from this behavior."

During the 1970s and into the 1980s, it was still acceptable for families to dump their special needs kids into facilities. This was for the good of the family. Or because no one expected a mom to be an expert of such matters. Or because a mom wasn't competent and the state had removed her children.

I was only 19 when I decided I needed to work at Hope House. I didn't have children of my own and had never worked with handicapped children.

I was designated competent after only a few hours of training.

Some children were runners. They sped through the halls in a fury as staff chased. Piles of adults, trying to control the violence, fell into mounds of flailing limbs. The child, pressed under the force of adults, screamed and cried and bit. Staff calmed the children through sheer force of will.

The kid stopped screaming when he or she was tired, but I didn't learn what the child was trying to tell us with this behavior. What was he or she trying to communicate? Was the child unhappy, or scared, or angry? Was it out of possibility that the crying and yelling and biting was not happiness run rampant? What was the child trying to tell us?

Despite this, it was still a shock when I had Nathan at age 21. I was too young for an American having a family, but the right age for a Mexican having children.

A few weeks after I gave birth, my husband left. He wasn't having fun. He didn't say this directly. Instead, he went out with other women who were willing to have fun. Women who were willing to put his needs first.

I don't love him. I couldn't handle the layers of lies stratifying our married lives together. I need to be a good mother. I need to raise a healthy child. I need to graduate college.

I need him to make room for who I want to be. I don't say any of these things. When he decides to leave, I help him pack.

Nathan doesn't respond to my voice. He can talk, but he won't. It expends too much energy, or it's too difficult, or perhaps his silence works for him. He isn't interested in connecting through words. He prefers to shake his head or shrug or makes sounds to answer.

The doctor says his ears work fine.

I sign Nathan up for school before he is ready. It's a class called pre-kinder, that's supposed to help kids who need extra support.

I'm vying for as much support as possible. The school assigns him a speech teacher and an adaptive PE teacher.

He's four and doesn't talk. The school hopes that with support, he'll talk. But I just want to communicate.

During a meeting, I ask, "Is sign language an option?"

"No," the speech teacher says, "that will enable this problem and discourage him from talking."

"Oh," I say, "I didn't know that."

I look away so she can't see my pain. I'm devastated. I can't connect with him. I'm desperate. But I don't say this. I don't think I know enough to have an opinion that overrides the speech teacher's.

He scratches his ears until his fingertips are thick with blood. His face is smeared with blood. Then his clothes, then me. I can't run the faucet over his hands. The water is severely stimulating, and I lose him completely. Our connection is very delicate.

Instead, I use a wipe and rub each finger while he squirms.

He hates school. He prefers the rhythm and security of home. The sounds at home are predicable. At school, the other kids are too loud and move too much. He shushes everyone and doesn't understand why they can't "just behave."

After the first week of kindergarten, the teacher meets me at the classroom door. She tells me he's a runner.

"Excuse me?" I say.

It sounds like fun, like childhood breaking into joyful gallops.

"He's a runner. We have to keep constant watch on him. He bolts out the door," she says.

She's my age. I know this because she was a cheerleader when we were in high school together. She was the kind of girl who sat on football player's laps and wore bright pink eye shadow. Now, she teaches kindergarten and wears Winnie-the-Pooh overalls.

I look at her, as I realize she is judging me. I'm embarrassed, but proud of his defiance, his willingness to pursue what he needs.

"I'm sorry," I say.

He runs out of the classroom. He doesn't have great coordination, but he gives himself fully to the run. Before the teacher realizes he is out of his seat, he is out the door. He races through the halls and reaches the parking lot.

The staff chases.

He's fully present in his body as he runs towards the parking lot. He did it! He got away. He looks around to formulate an escape plan. As he pauses to breathe in rough sobs, they catch him.

The teacher catches him. She's called for help. It's an emergency! A kid has escaped and is headed into the street.

For him, it's an opportunity to be away from the misery of other children.

He could be home right now. He's a child wired to react. The school simply doesn't understand what he is telling them. As he is forcefully taken back to the classroom, his fingers catch the frame. He screams and howls like a cat about to be thrown into a well—while the teachers talk to him and coo and teach him about conformity.

Drowning is silent. The lungs fill with water and screaming becomes impossible. That isn't the case with Nathan. He struggles and fights all the way through.

As I watch him drowning in his own senses, I feel that there is nothing I can do.

Nathan's brain and senses don't speak the same language. There is a wiring issue that tangles the way they talk to one another. His nose smells citrus, but his brain translates it into waves of pain that cause him to grab violently at his nose. He slams onto the floor as if he's hit a wall. He begins to scream and cry, overwhelmed.

I don't understand. I'm doing everything right, right?

Being in the shower feels like bullets shooting at his skin. He twists in pain. Screaming. Screaming. Until the pain takes away his screams and violent shaking takes over. He shrinks under the shower until he is on the floor of the tub.

"This doesn't feel good," he means.

But I'm scrambling in fright, trying to figure out what's gone wrong.

What am I doing wrong?

All the information coming in simultaneously causes a traffic jam in his head. He tries but can't work through all the stuff coming in at once. It comes easy to some of us. We can distinguish smells and sounds and movement, and separate the information they are trying to give us. It doesn't send us into meltdowns.

He copes as best he can.

I don't change the showerhead again.

I can see his courage. He's a hard worker, tenacious. He's drowning in his own senses, but he stays afloat.

The school decides he is retarded. They don't know enough about alternative forms of communication or alternatives ways of being a person. They've measured his vocabulary. They've measured his speech. He isn't scoring well. He must be stupid.

"He's not retarded," I say. I'm gentle when I think the school is trying to help. I think we are working together. I'm trying to bridge their understanding.

I'm the bridge again.

I photocopy information to hand out during meetings. I'm naïve.

"He's not retarded!" I yell when I realize he's an unmanageable problem the school doesn't want. He's expensive and impacts their test scores.

My words are sharp and angry and as loud as a gesture.

What I mean is: I'm alone and afraid. I don't know what to do.

But I don't say this. Saying it aloud might make it real. It might dissolve my world.

It's worse when he's eight. He's still struggling. He can't read body language or facial expressions. Norms aren't for him. He prefers a direct approach. The social niceties so relevant and important to others escape him like water cupped in a hand.

He doesn't pretend he likes his teacher. He doesn't pretend he has friends. He doesn't pretend he isn't lonely.

The loneliness is the worst part.

Despite the sounds and sensations he has to grapple with to reach understanding, he knows he is different. He knows he is alone. He doesn't feign happiness.

And I can't either.

When I'm called into the office because he's bit another child, I go in with an attitude.

"He bit another child," the principal says.

I know my son. He isn't violent.

"Was the kid being an asshole?"

I look pleasant enough. It shocks people when I'm direct, when I cuss.

"Well, yes. He was bullying Nathan. He called Nathan stupid. He pushed Nathan and Nathan bit him."

"It sounds like the kid deserved it."

"Maybe," he says.

"I'll talk to Nathan, but I expect you to do your job and protect him."

I walk out with as much pride as I can. Nathan does the same. When the principal asks him to wait to be walked back to class, Nathan speaks for the first time during that meeting.

"Thank you. I can find my own way back."

The principal is shocked and tumbles after him.


I start thinking about dignity differently. Who's it for and how do you maintain and nurture it for yourself and others? What if dignity turns into bites?

I desperately want to hug him. But he doesn't like this. We begin a ritual that lasts throughout his teens and into his twenties. I grasp his pinkie with my pinkie. This act, this understanding, this connection fills him with joy. He makes a happy, squeaky sound at our touch.

My arms still itch to fold him into me. But he's not there to fulfill my needs. I'm there to fulfill his.

Unlike other kids, Nathan doesn't yawn. Yawning is an act of empathy that means you are connecting with others. He learns to yawn in order to fit in. I explain to him that yawning is not a gesture like a shrug. It's an involuntary act.

"But I'm tired," he says.

"Yea, but that's not the way yawning works."

He's a runner into high school.

He changes his technique. His reasons become more complicated. He changes how he explains it.

Because he doesn't relate to the outside world the way I do, he has no idea I've been tracking his behavior. I can see the pattern, deep, ingrained, and unending, the way water works into the earth.

When he is still running in middle school, I change what I believe and how I see his actions. What is he telling me?

In high school, I give up on trying to make it work within a regular school system. My husband and I hire an advocate and fight to get him into a special needs school. He begins to date almost immediately. He falls in love. He makes friends and becomes obscenely popular. He finds his voice there. He's still not a talker, but he hits his groove.

In 2016, while I am helping a friend do deep research to help advocate for a child with special needs, I first hear the term "selective mutism." It feels like I've been hit in the face with a turd. But I remember my training. I don't react.

Steven's dad is sitting across from me. My friend sits next to him. It's taken her 12 years to get him to advocate for his son. She was Steven's caregiver when he was a baby. Steven is 16 years old and his best friend is a stuffed animal. He only eats red foods. His mom didn't have the courage to show up to our meeting. I understand this.

"Mi esposa…" the man explains.

"It's okay," I say in Spanish, "we all do what we can. I'm glad that you are here."

I do this on a voluntary basis. Most parents can't take action on the advice I give. They are in too much pain. What they want when I sit in front of them is for the pain to go away. They need someone to listen to how difficult this is.

I take notes and ask Steven's dad a million questions. I work backwards. I read the last Individual Education Plan (IEP), then the one before that and the one before. It takes me hours to go through the piles of papers. When I finally turn to the first IEP, I see it there, written.

There. That thing that stood between my son and I. That thing that made me understand dignity better. That helped me find my own humanity and empathy—that forced me to find my voice and wrestle with my isolation.

That forced me to confront my rage.

That stole my right to be shy.

That thing that broke my voice down into raw sounds—
alongside my son.

The first IEP reads, "Potential autism."

# Tiger Says Meow

I WALKED INTO THAT SMALL classroom, stopping at the door to glance around. There were 10 children and their aides in there. The school day had already started. The district had called me last minute when the aide assigned to one of the children had called in sick.

There were six aides in the classroom. One of the special needs aides had announced upon arriving that she had a headache and was already 30 minutes into a nap.

If there was a teacher in the classroom, I could not immediately distinguish her from the rest of the aides. I looked for nicer shoes and an air of extra confidence. Then I looked for the white woman in the group.

"The teacher just stepped out to make copies," said a male aide, "can I help you?"

"I'm with David today," I said.

"That's him over there," said the aide.

He pointed to a scrawny kid with dark hair and a lean face.

"He can talk. But he's mainly non-verbal," said the aide. "He's a cool kid. He likes to run out to the bathroom, so keep an eye on him. Don't let him out of the classroom. It's hard to get him back in."

I taught elementary school in the 1990s when I was in my early twenties. By the time I was in my late twenties, the disappointments of working in a system that cares more about the teachers and the money than the children broke me. But I wasn't ready to stop working to create lasting change in children's lives.

I applied for and got a position at the Los Angeles Unified School District's (LAUSD) Program, Evaluation and Research Branch collecting data from classrooms for the researchers at LAUSD to analyze. In this new position, I observed classrooms for six hours at a time, took copious notes, and made a supported decision about whether or not the classroom was teaching English Language Acquisition. In 2005, when work slowed in our department, I decided to help a fellow co-worker on the Modified Consent Decree at the Los Angeles Unified School District.

The Modified Consent Decree came out of a legal decision to monitor Special Education services in the district. In 1993, Chanda Smith's parents sued LAUSD for not meeting the needs of their child. The Chanda Smith plaintiffs wanted LAUSD to comply with federal law that says all children deserve an equal educational opportunity. In 1996, Chanda Smith's counsel and LAUSD drew up the Consent Decree: a list of recommendations to help LAUSD to comply with federal standards. Eventually, quantifiable measures were added, leading to the Modified Consent Decree. This was a list of standards the district had to meet with special needs students to be in compliance. Our team was there to monitor the progress.

At the time I was hired for this position, my son was 10 years old. He had non-specific undiagnosed special needs. I'd had him tested at various places. I was a single mom, working two jobs, and barely had money to get through the week. But I had him tested, paying out of pocket. I was desperate. I felt frustrated and disempowered and angry. With this project, at least I could ensure that some special needs kids were getting services.

The Modified Consent Decree covered all special needs services. We didn't have the capacity to look at each service to evaluate its quality. We decided to find out whether the services were actually taking place according to each child's Individual Education Plan (IEP). As the name implies, each IEP is specific to each child's needs. The IEP acts as a legal document that the school has to comply with.

In 2005, I was in the classroom to see if the district was providing the interventions they'd agreed to provide. Until 1975, many schools were not even teaching special education children on the same campus as mainstream ("regular") students. Every child is different, but the United States promises that all children have the right to a free public education. In other words, all children in the community have an equal access to schooling no matter their race, ethnicity, religion, socio-economic status, sexual orientation or documentation. This applies to special needs kids as much as it does to all other children.

I found myself in a project where I was watching while students received their services, whatever they might be.

In research, watching is what you primarily do when you collect data. There is no intervening, no commenting, no talking and no advising. There is only watching. Eventually, watching depressed me. I needed action. I needed to be able to create change.

I decided to take a position as a special needs aide in my spare time. I thought it would fill the void and helplessness I felt while observing. I applied to another district and received a position.

To the untrained eye, the classroom I walked into looked like any other elementary class. Except this classroom was filled to capacity with special needs children. It's what they call, in California, a "self-contained classroom." It's a plonking ground for all special needs children who can't be part of a regular education classroom. They are all put in the same classroom despite age and diagnosis.

When you put a special education kid in regular classrooms it's called "mainstreaming" or "inclusion." These labels always bother me. It's as if there really is a main tributary where we are trying to "include" everyone who isn't like the dominant population. It's like watching schools trying to turn all cats into grey tabbies.

It's a ridiculous situation. The principal decides the school's vision. The staff follow. What happens between the construction and delivery of that message, and how the staff views it and enacts it is a whole different situation. In the meantime, the principal wants grey tabbies and the teachers try frantically to paint stripes on all the children in order to meet the standards.

Except that special needs children, despite their diagnoses, defy labels.

I hadn't been trained but my 11-year-old son has autism like David, and I wasn't intimidated. In fact, I was angry about the conditions in the classroom. On first glance, I could tell the materials and assignments weren't right for the kids.

Most people assume that all children should be learning the same thing in an American classroom. But math and phonemes aren't always the solution to our special needs children. Often, they are desperately in need of social skills. They don't know how to identify or label the things they feel. They need help with this more than they need to understand what letter "cat" begins with.

The art assignment the classroom teacher had designed for them wasn't working. The children ate paste in globs while the aides tried to get through this. The children struggled to sit in chairs and focus on the given assignment. They didn't have the motor skills to work scissors and struggled to cut. They struggled with spreading the paste.

And I struggled to understand the inanity of the assignment. Who was winning here?

David eyed the exit. I could see by the way he rocked slightly that he was up to mischief. I blocked his exit with my body so he couldn't escape to the bathroom. I distracted him with a marble game.

Many children with autism love to build. David loved building a maze that he ran marbles through, a series of loops and trails. The marble always ended up in the same place, but it didn't matter to David. He loved the motion.

Eventually, I missed the open door. But David didn't. He ran down the small hall and into the bathroom. He squealed as he laughed. Once in the bathroom, he ran and got himself into a stall. Thinking that he needed to use the bathroom, I initially waited patiently. Till the flushing started. Once, then twice, then again.

"David, are you okay? Do you need help?" I said.

David flushed again. He screamed in happiness.

I walked into the stall. He was having the best time of his life. He was flushing and running away from the bathroom. His body was curled inward as he covered his ears and shrieked with glee.

His joy was amazing.

I pulled him back into the classroom. He was resistant but he came along. I was sorry I dragged him back. Like him, I could see that the bathroom was more fun than the art activity.

The rest of the time, David would ask "Tiger says?" and respond to himself "Meow." He thought this was hilarious. The fact is, I did too. I wondered how he had arrived at such a funny narrative. Had he made up the joke himself?

You don't put children in a self-contained classroom unless you have to. In a public school, it's the most restrictive place you can put a child, doubly so if they also have an adult monitoring them at all times. Someone had decided David couldn't survive in a regular class and had placed him in a classroom with children who ate paste. Meanwhile, I wondered at his brilliance. In the right setting, he could be a comedian. In the right setting, he might be able to able to thrive and have friends.

The warmth and authenticity of special needs kids is an amazing thing. In 2017, during a workshop at the Regional Center, a resource center for special needs children in California, a presenting social worker said to us, "I am better than Brendan at math or at tying my shoes. I'm good at these skills. But I can see that he is a better human than I am. He's honest. He's more human than I can ever hope to be. In this aspect, he's better than me. But this humanity isn't what they are measured for. We don't have an assessment for this."

You can't compare one human to another. When it comes to autism, we just don't understand enough to even begin such a comparison. We can't even compare one autistic person to another. People always ask, "Is your child high-functioning?" That doesn't mean anything. Functioning how or where?

The Regional Center measures each child's intellect, but they also measure the child's capacity to discern when they are unsafe, to cook for themselves, and make general decisions about their well-being. They want to know if the child will eventually be able to live alone and take care of themselves.

But how does an adult with special needs navigate a world that has already decided they are not enough? How did David go to school everyday understanding that he was going to be measured by his failures again and again? By placing him in a room with all the other "misfits", his brilliance was muted. He was lumped into the unusual and therefore, dismissed.

The system fails them and yet they still have to figure out how to live, how to get by, how to thrive.

My son is 23 years old now. He went to school every day with dread, understanding that he would be told in great detail everything he was doing wrong. The school he attended in elementary grades didn't even like how he held his pencil. When he was initially diagnosed, they told me he would never be able to read.

He reads. He's figuring out how to take care of himself and is in love with a woman he's been with for over four years. He's training to record and engineer sound for movies and television. He's accomplished things I never thought he would, not because he and I didn't work hard, but because the schools told us both to accept his limitations.

For many years, the fact that he lived in his own mind, in the safety of his own head, was understood by schools to be stupidity. But he was blatantly aware of what the schools thought. He wasn't making eye contact, but he knew he was different and undervalued. He knew the schools had written him off. And you know what? He'd written them off, too. By the time Nathan was 10 years old, he had already decided that schools weren't worth his time.

I'm very proud of Nathan. Like David, Nathan has a great sense of humor. We've attended social skills programs that have tried to teach Nathan not to be funny, not to tell jokes. At that time, programs were afraid that kids would make themselves targets if they tried to be humorous. But Nathan never conformed. He was sure of who he was. In 2017, he put together a film where he stars as the main character, who is called upon to be a superhero.

I sat with the audience and watched him on the big screen. My eyes widened with wonder at the complexity of his story, and I wondered how he had managed to put it together during a time when he'd been suffering a horrible mental break.

In his movie, he stumbles around, trying to be a hero, bumping into things, misunderstanding, and falling apart, even as he's called upon to save the world. His movie was unexpected in its storyline and humor.

It's true that sometimes we are called to be heroes. This goes for all of us. The call for heroes isn't stingy or discriminatory. The call is there for anyone who cares to answer it. Sometimes that hero roars its response. It is loud and dominating and makes everyone tremble with the fear of its power. But sometimes that hero, that tiger, says meow.

# Autism in Lust

**Fourteen**

HE'S SUDDENLY DATING, AFTER telling me girls don't interest him. A bold girl put her mouth on his, and he's giddy with emotion.

"So, is she your girlfriend now? What's going on?" I say.

"I don't know. But you might be a grandma soon."

He says this with a swagger. He must have picked that up from anime or cartoons. I never know what he will pull out from what I call his "bag of tricks." He's bagged and collected a series of phrases and gestures ready to be used—like Felix the Cat, ready to disarm.

I am a young mom. His words land on me like a fire poker. But it's never good to be reactionary when it comes to Nathan. I wait and think, instead.

At bedtime, I go to his room to say good night. He's sitting upright on his bed. I gesture for him to move over, I sit next to him.

"Yeah, so do you feel ready for sex?" I say.

"What? No!"

"Oh. You said earlier that I might be a grandma soon, and you make babies with sex. So, I thought you might be ready to have sex. If that's the case, I thought we should talk. The girl you kissed, is she ready for sex?"

"No! We just kissed."

He avoids my eyes. He crosses his arms over the blanket, frowns and pouts his mouth to show distaste.

"Okay. So, um…You make babies through sex. You can prevent babies if you use a condom."

"I *know!*"

He scoffs at me indignantly and turns away. I've unsettled his dignity. I've shaken up his self-perception of coolness.

"Um, what's a condom?"

We have someone coming to the house once a week to teach sex ed. Why in the world hasn't he discussed birth control?

"I need to call your instructor. He's supposed to have talked to you about condoms. Did he talk about condoms?"

"I don't know," he says.

"How can you not know? You were there. Are you paying attention?"

"No."

"You just ignore him when he talks to you?"

"Yes."

"This sucks," I say.

## Twenty-one

I am sitting cross-legged on the floor, reviewing a report for work. He comes into the living room. He's taller than any kid I thought I'd ever have. He's all arms and legs and despite his age, he seems forever unaware of the space his body takes up.

"I'm ready to get laid," he says.

The words are fast and mumbled. It's almost as if he doesn't want me to hear what he needs to say. But this doesn't make sense. Perhaps, he's hoping I catch a vibe that leads me to understanding. He doesn't like to explain things. His thinking is primarily visual. As he thinks, he sees things in pictures in his mind that relate to what he knows and that relate to something else. For him, it's like watching a slideshow. Then he interprets these images to make meaning. My brain doesn't work this way. Things come at me like puzzles and I prefer not to make assumptions. I unravel things carefully, like unwrapping a gift from Ted Kaczynski- the Unabomber. I need him to help me build understanding.

"Excuse me? What?" I say.

He sways nervously from side to side. He sighs. Then stares at me, his eyes big. He doesn't like eye contact. The contact is temporary and fleeting. I might not see his gaze again for a long while.

"I'm sorry," I say. "Do you mean sex? Are we talking about sex?"

I'm trying to stay calm. I used to teach sex ed. I'm unafraid of the talk. Vagina. Penis. Whatever. I'm comfortable with the mechanics of mating. It's the other stuff that confounds me: the feeling, the regret, the need for aberration or conformity. I don't like to deal with the ethics. And it's about to become ethical if he's thinking about having sex with another person.

"Yes," he says.

"Okay."

He's a night talker, and I have a deadline. But he only approaches me if he has something to say. Otherwise, he mumbles or uses one-word responses. He prefers gestures and guttural sounds. I set the report aside. He takes this as a signal and sits down on the rug next to me.

"What's going on?" I say.

"I'm ready to have sex."

"I understand that. What's this got to do with me?"

"Can I have sex?"

"You're an adult. You don't need my permission. Do you have someone in mind for sex?"

"Yes."

"Is it your girlfriend?"

"Yes."

"Does she know you are thinking about sex?"

"I don't know."

"I think you need to talk to her. That's where you start."

I look away, thinking the conversation is over. Perhaps he just needed direction and a confirmation that he's an adult? He's quiet. Is he ruminating, or processing, or trying to deepen the conversation?

"Okay. What do I do?" he says.

I'm staying calm. Goodness, how am I staying calm? I take a deep breath. I'm going to have to deal with his girlfriend's mom. I don't like that. She'll call or text me. She'll want to know why my son is putting his penis in their precious girl. Mothers of special needs daughters are a special breed. They are demanding, insisting, unreasonable, and explosive. They seem to both want their daughters to lead normal lives, while at once hoping their daughters never have to see a penis. The enormity of having to deal with this hits me. He'll struggle if he has to do this alone.

"I was really hoping not be involved in your sex life," I say. "I guess we should start with the legalities. Is she conserved?"

"I don't know."

"You need to figure out whether she has legal rights to do whatever she wants with her body first."

"Okay. Then what?"

"Then, you need to figure out whether she wants sex."

"I think she does."

"I think you need to ask her. But also, do you have indications that she might want to have sex? Have you deeply kissed or touched her breasts and have you touched her in, other, more intimate places?"

"Yes. We—"

"No, no! Don't tell me. If you have and if she has touched you, then you might be able to ask her about going further. When couples are hoping to have sex, these are some of the clues they look for. But really, you just need to have a conversation with her."

"Okay."

He leaves the room. I can't concentrate on my report anymore. I go to bed instead.

The next day, he comes back to me.

"She said okay. Now what do I do?"

"Seriously, dude?" I say.

"Yeah."

"Um, okay..."

**Twenty-two**

It's been three days since he had sex with his girlfriend. I'm at work. My phone is ringing. He's supposed to be on the bus to his training program. He rarely calls me. He doesn't like to talk over the phone. It's usually texts with short words and lots of emoticons.

"What's up?" I say.

He's listening for my tone. If I sound annoyed, he won't continue. He'll say he just called to say "hi." We both know he doesn't do that. But if he decides to opt out because of my tone, we'll both hang up and pretend he just called to say "hi."

"Is it scientifically proven that there is no cure for autism?" he says.

I know what's coming and I laugh nervously.

"Yes. There is no cure. What's going on?"

"I think sex cured my autism."

I feel a hysterical laugh rising within me. I smother it down. He hates it if I laugh at him when he's telling me something serious. He never sees it as anything but ridicule.

"I think that's a relatively normal reaction. You feel relaxed. You would feel something similar if you exercised or if you meditated."

"Really?"

"Yes, really."

I want to lecture him about how I've been pushing both exercise and meditation for years. I don't do that. I'm struggling to be a better listener myself. I pull away from the damage my criticism would cost us both. I want to protect him and arm him. I try to give him what he needs instead of what I need.

A few days later, I am in the kitchen. I'm cooking white beans in a slow cooker, adding broth and herbs. I imagine the buttery taste of the beans in my mouth. He comes in and rests his body against the wall and leans forward to rest his forearms on the back of the kitchen chair.

"STDs don't run in our family, so I'm good right?"

I stop myself from laughing.

"The men in our family are whores. They probably have all kinds of STDs. That's not the point, though, because that's not how STDs work. You need to use a condom to prevent STDs."

"Oh. Okay," he says.

"Did you use a condom? Do you need help figuring out condoms?"

"No!"

"Okay. Use a condom. It'll help prevent diseases. It's the only thing that can."

"Okay. When do I get to have sex again?" he says.

"Why are you asking me? I'm not the person you are having sex with."

"Oh."

A few days after our STD talk, we are driving together in the car. He's refused to be in the front seat with me. He's in the back seat listening to his phone.

This is the second time we have driven out to look for homes. Our regional center is helping us find a mentor family that Nathan can live with. I'm hopeful that this mentor home will work out. The first mentor family felt like a great fit for us, but when we calculated the travel via bus from Whittier to Glendale, we were horrified to see that travel would be three hours each way to Nathan's vocational program.

This household is much closer to his program, but they have three dogs. Dogs make him anxious. Their energy is too high for him, constant movement, constant need, constant noise. He prefers cats of the non-asshole variety.

Our social worker is already there when we arrive. The woman who answers the door is small, squat, and leather skinned. We get an immediate tour of the house. She's anxious. Nathan would be her first special needs occupant. She's only had experience with foster children. She peppers her conversation with constant apologies. When we finally sit down, our host tells us about her dogs. We can hear them in the other room, yipping, and trying to dig their way out.

I hold my breath as she goes to open her bedroom door. They are a storm of aggressive need. She's a collector of things that need. In this instance, it's dogs, but this clearly also includes young people. For all I know, she collects spoons and hapless men who don't have homes. She mentions a boyfriend.

The dogs look around frantically. Nathan stiffens but pretends he is unaffected.

"Are you okay?" I whisper.

"Yes. Of course, I'm okay."

I can tell he's not okay. But I'm not going to shred his dignity with my doubts.

Our host tells us how she got the dogs and why she loves them. The dogs ignore our host's profession of love. Instead, they begin to sniff the unknown people and nip at each other in dominance, before their aggressive need to love and dominate turns itself over and they start to mate.

For the next 30 minutes, the dogs fuck. I'm appalled at their unabashed stamina and ability to hump over and over again. Nathan is trying not to look at them. I'm trying to focus on the conversation at hand. I do what I do when I'm stressed. I pull myself inside my head, where my imagination can keep me entertained for hours. But the social worker is asking me a question.

"I'm sorry. Can you repeat that?"

"I wondered if Nathan can take his medication on his own."

"Yes," I say. "He does that on his own."

The dogs haven't stopped.

"I love your red lamp," I say to our host. "I used to have a lamp like that. It had this beautiful silk lampshade."

"I'm active!" Nathan says.

Time slows as I scramble to understand how lamps fit into Nathan's statement. Shit. Is he going to start talking about his sex life this openly?

I panic and my mouth goes dry.

"Are you? Are we talking about this now?" I say.

"Yes."

"Seriously? Right now."

I'm trying to buy myself time. I'm going to have to account for this. He won't have the words to advocate for himself. He'll need me.

"Yes," he says.

He's sure. He's confident. All I can think of is how the dogs were mating and my son just yelled out the equivalent of: "I do that, too!"

Thankfully, the social worker takes the reins for a bit. She's asking clarifying questions and validating Nathan's experience. I take that moment to glance at our host. She's horrified and that makes me angry. She can't believe he's sexually active.

"No. We can't have that," the host says, "We're women. This is a household with *women*."

I start cautiously, "Nathan has been dating the same girl for four years. Their relationship has become sexual."

Nathan is beaming. He loves his new sexuality.

"I think all people have a right to have closeness with one another. Intimacy isn't something that should be reserved for certain people. I'm aware and support the fact that he is having sex."

"Yes." Our host looks like she's hoping to burrow out of this conversation.

"But we're women," she says.

"And Nathan has the right, just like everyone else, to be a sexual person," I say.

"Yes, of course. But he can't do that here."

I stop. We end our conversation with a few niceties. I can't wait to get out of that place, where dogs can have sex and our host can have sex with her boyfriend who stays overnight.

"Thank you for your time," I say as we leave.

Our social worker trails after us.

"She actually can't prevent him from having company," she says.

"We'll be in touch with you," I say to her.

Nathan and I pile back into the car. Again, he chooses the backseat. He settles into place and puts on his headphones. For a few minutes, we disconnect from the world. I take deep breaths and listen to the radio as my imagination runs wild. I think about how I ended up here. I question my decisions. I'm annoyed by Nathan's boldness but impressed by his courage to be only who he is. I like him. But the rawness of who he is always hits me the same way; looking at him is like looking into a bright light. He is ablaze in his humanity.

# Breaking Bolillo

OUR MEETING SPACE WAS A clinic during the day. A non-profit had hired me to consult on a community research project. The parents streamed in with their children. They gathered in the reception area around two joined tables surrounded by chairs. Then came into the nurses' station to grab dinner.

I was already at the nurses' station, splitting a bolillo with my thumbs. I balanced the plate with the bread on my left hand, while I filled it with beans and a chunk of fresh cheese. Then bumbled to open the salsa container.

A woman with fierce eyes grabbed a plate and got in line to get food.

"Buenas noches. I'm Mireya," I said.

"Martha. Buenas noches," she said.

She was short and had a pinched mouth with downturned lines.

"I don't know what it is about eating with community. The food always tastes better," I said. I didn't elaborate. I didn't know if she remembered me from when I observed this group two years ago.

"You know what they say," she said, "the taco that isn't yours is always the tastiest. That's why there is so much infidelity."

I was unsure whether to laugh. The conversation had taken a raunchy turn. Before, I could say anything she continued, "Let me tell you about my lover."

I put my food down on the plate to look at her. I squared my shoulders with hers and offered my respectful silence.

It's difficult in poor Latino communities to have meetings without food and childcare. Most community meetings consist of women, and women come with children. Providing food and childcare is a nod to parents. It says that you understand cultural norms. Most of all, food is a language in this space. It's a welcome mat. It says: *I see you. I understand your needs and value your time. Please come eat with me and talk.*

I'd coached the project leads for four years. Two years ago, when we started the data collection part of the project, I met with the parents and was struck by the violence. We were trying to come up with a good research question the women could use to empower their civic engagement. But the more I listened, the more alarmed I felt. I stopped the entire conversation and asked them to raise their hand if they had experienced violence outside their homes in the past six months.

They all raised their hands. They each talked about being attacked and handled by strangers. I immediately turned to the organizers.

"You have to address this," I said.

"We don't have time," one organizer said, "and we don't have the resources."

"You can't ignore this," I said. "This is a social justice issue. Trauma tends to leak all over everything. It's hard to stay objective if your life has been impacted by trauma. You need to do your best to take care of it."

"We will try, but we don't have the funding."

Now, here we were, two years later. The project was about to end. The trauma wasn't addressed. This was evident in the hard turn this project had taken. The women wanted to clean up the streets. They wanted the streets to look safe and feel safe. But they were blinded by their fears. They remembered being attacked by men on the streets. These homeless men on the streets looked dangerous. They wanted these people gone.

"Why?" I asked.

"They don't belong here," one community member said.

"But then, where do they belong?"

No one answered.

"I have a family member that is homeless," I said, "He had a very abusive childhood. His dad was very violent. This family member ended up committing crimes. He did jail time. He got out and committed more crimes. He did more jail time. Now, he's homeless. His family is afraid of him. But he started out as a child in need that no one helped. Whose fault was that? Not his. There should have been help for him."

There was silence. Some women nodded. Then the strong rejections arose.

"They are alcoholics. God hates that."

"They have no business being homeless."

"That person shouldn't have been bad."

I was appalled. I see homelessness as a result of unresolved issues—a symptom of societal failure. I believe that most of us are on the verge of being homeless.

It was too late to try to change the group's collective understanding of homelessness. But I had to try.

I'd been a researcher for 14 years. I tried to be a good listener. Data collectors and clients often complained about how Latinos can't answer structured questions.

When women are wading knee deep in trauma, all they can do is give that trauma a narrative and tell it as a story. Trauma doesn't have a timeline. The enormous effort it takes to place flashes of visuals and emotions in chronological order is staggering.

It's my job as a researcher to figure out what that story means.

As Martha told me about her lover, I listened intently for the layers in her story. I could immediately gather a couple of things. I could tell she was testing me. She was trying to figure out if I was safe or a prude who didn't understand the issues. She was trying to shock me, perhaps claim the space. I was a stranger to her, dressed like a repressed researcher, or what most Americans called "office casual". Needless to say, my sexuality was tampered down and bound by a sensible bra, a pair of slacks and practical shoes.

"I'm married," she said, "I've been married to the same man for over 20 years." Her face crumbled in distaste. "We have kids together. My mom picked him out for me when I was crossing the border. She said I was unlikely to get raped if I chose a man to protect me."

I heard the logic, but also understood the pain of leaving a homeland that was crushing you to enter a country that didn't want you. Her mom's logic was practical. Over 80% of women crossing the border get raped.

I could imagine her mom assessing the men waiting to cross the border. I imagined her thinking her daughter might be split like a bolillo to feed the hunger of them all. So, she picked the meanest looking man. *That one*, she said to her 15-year-old daughter.

"I've been with him ever since. We had kids. Then I met this guy. And oh my, he is so wonderful. He treats me so well and invites me out to movies. I've been seeing him for a while."

She's flushed and waves her hands in front of her heated face.

"Are you in love with this new guy?" I asked.

"Yes," she said, "yes."

I threw my arms around her.

"I'm so glad you are in love," I said. "You deserve that."

She held me fiercely and we rocked each other gently, before she grabbed her food, and I grabbed mine.

# Touch : Tocar

AT 12 YEARS OLD, AFTER I had started menstruating, Mother warned me never to be alone with men. I needed to hide my body. She was ashamed of my body and hers. She thought women and their female functions were disgusting.

But when she talked about marriage and connection, I thought there might be more than this—more than burden, sorrow, and regret. Perhaps the female body was hallowed. Women were sacred. Their bodies were sacred—and their bodies were covered with a text only their husbands could read.

Our women only got one shot at marriage. Happiness didn't matter. Self-worth didn't matter. Validation didn't matter. What mattered is that only their husband shared the written word of their body. If marriages failed, our women spent their lives alone. They stayed on the shelf, dusty and unread.

In 1994, my maternal grandmother cooked in the hazy light of morning in Mexico. Every other day, she dragged out her tortilla table. She poured flour into a plastic bowl. She added lard and salt, then water. She squeezed the lard and flour between her palms. She worked silently this way until she had a round mass. She broke that mass into smaller round balls that she patted into disks with her fingers. She scooped flour with her hand and spread it across the table. She turned to the comal. She checked the flame and pressed her bare fingers on the hot surface to see if it was ready. She reached for her rolling pin and pressed it over a disk of dough. The flour spread across the table; some of it incorporated into the dough. The rest dusted her hands and arms.

She began the rhythm of making tortillas. Her rolling pin knocked on the table and scraped the tortillas thin.

The flour powdered her in white. Her arms were marked with burns and injuries; both current and from years past. Her veins were a stark purple, visible between other spots of color. The landscape of her flesh was a mix of her own pink skin, angry red burns, and brown age spots.

She was alone. She lived in a house-full of people but she was alone. She played her part as the matriarch, mother, and wife. She made those tortillas. Even after not speaking to her husband for 20 years, she made sure he ate.

Grandfather lived in a separate home across the small patio from the main house. I thought for many years that she refused to share a house with him, but he had decided to live separately.

They'd had eight children together. Three had died as babies. Their mutual experiences bound them. Their bodies had been intimately connected. But now, they couldn't even lock eyes.

I didn't have to wonder how alone that felt. I knew, but I also understood that loneliness comes in many flavors. I wondered how her loneliness compared to mine.

"No seas tonta. Nunca sabes quien te va tocar," my Tía Lupe started saying to me when I was 14 years old.

This mantra bound us. Her words rang like a beat in my bones when I was married, like the kind of buzzing that vibrated my body after it was slammed up against a wall. My shoulders hit first, then the back of my head bounced, cracking the plaster. The buzzing continued until the adrenalin kicked in. The pain was absent then. The pain would come later, after the fear caught up. But at that moment, shoved against a wall, I wrapped my arms around my pregnant belly and tried to curl into a tight ball. To make myself small.

My husband yelled, "Look what you are making me do!"

In 1994, I was 21 and divorced for the first time.

The marriage wasn't working for me. The violence hurt. The betrayals hurt more. I couldn't trust him enough to touch me.

When my husband left me, my son was two weeks old. I'd only been married six months. In six months, he had left four times. He kept a bag packed in our room. I'm not sure if he expected me to unpack it and beg him to stay, but I wasn't that kind of woman.

"Leave if you want," I said.

"I'm not coming back!"

"If you leave again, you don't get to come back," I said.

"You're just going to throw away what we have?" he said.

"I'm not the one that's leaving."

He expected tears. He expected begging. But I was holding a baby in my arms and the weight of the child far outweighed anything else. I couldn't bother with a childish

235

man who couldn't be faithful and couldn't commit to what I thought we were building together.

In the years that span the life my grandmother spent with my grandfather, she loved him. He stuck around and he expected his steady presence to be enough. This wasn't enough for her. She wanted him to be devoted. She wanted him to work hard for her and for the family. She wanted his love to cost him as much as it had cost her. His rejection grew alive between them.

Because of the way she loved, she left her family as a young girl to be with him. In that part of Mexico, the mail was slow and contact wasn't secure. She left her family knowing she might not see them again.

After they were married, she lost babies. Her first, second, and fourth children died. And when my mom was four years old, my grandmother left to the United States and worked in a factory. My grandfather couldn't or wouldn't work and she wouldn't let the family starve. In the United States, she must have felt alone. The loneliness felt like a massive weight. I'm convinced that's why her spine curved with osteoporosis.

The pain on her back, as it curved, must have been even lonelier.

Tocar is a funny word. In Spanish, it means "to touch," but it also means to play, to finger. It refers to contact and, depending on how you use it, it has implications of both sensuality and violence. When the women in my family wondered "Quien te va tocar?" they wondered who I would end up with. In marriage. I hoped it meant more than that. I hoped it meant "Who will touch you?" Who will move you? Who will make you sing?

I hoped that marriage would provide intimacy and connection—that when my husband touched me, it would be with love. I wondered whether the women in my family had wanted the same for themselves.

What I didn't know is that marriage is a long term commitment that takes more than touch. I thought a union with someone just happened. I thought it had a lot to do with luck, with chance, with what you deserved.

I've wondered if the women in my family thought that, too. That it was a luck of the draw.

Our women chose poor life partners. My mom was unhappily married to my father. My Tía Frencis was a single mother who never married. My Tía Lupe was married to a horribly violent person. Her mom, my Tía Belia was alone. She'd been married to a man who had beat her for 20 years. Instead of thinking about marriage, she pondered her safety and her willingness to live.

The immediacy and temperature of love made it difficult to see who this man might become in 10 or 20 years. Or our women lacked imagination. Perhaps they had not heard the narratives around them that taught the grueling pace of love, the burnout. Perhaps believing in the sanctity of the female body, they also thought they were beyond logic and common sense. This belief in sanctity brought them closer to god. This belief made them think that god might treat them well. That if they followed god, they might have a better life.

"No seas tonta. Nunca sabes quien te va tocar," my Tía Lupe said to me when I was 15 years old.

"¿Porque te casaste?" I said.

"Por mensa. Le creí lo que me dijo. Los hombres dicen cosas bonitas," she said.

Was the chemistry fickle? Or the dedication? Or were men truly filled with lies? When did god just leave you alone to deal with this? Or was god a man too?

I saw my grandmother eight months after my first divorce, while visiting in Mexico.

"That marriage didn't count," she said. "He wasn't even Catholic."

I held her arm as we walked towards the back entrance of her house. She said this to me quietly. The other women in the family walked behind us. In line, or arm in arm, the way they were supposed to, hanging on to the rules our matriarch, my grandmother, had instilled in them.

She loved me, and I knew she was trying to expand the rules for me. The rest of the women were alone. They worked difficult jobs and came home to their children. If they were privileged to have a husband, they might not have to work. But the others worked themselves raw. They tiptoed around Grandmother, trying not to let her in on separations or divorces. Why did I deserve any different?

My grandmother passed away when my son was four. I broke down with grief. No one had loved me the way that she did. No one would love me like that again.

I also remember the loneliness of never being touched. I remember the loneliness of not being able to touch my son, who had special needs and didn't like the sensation of other people's hands on him. But more than anything, I remember the lack of connection with anyone.

I wondered how all the women had done this. Did they all feel as alone as I felt? I wanted big things, but I also just needed to not feel alone in the decisions I was making for my son. I was making medical and school decisions and I wasn't even sure if they were right. I didn't feel like I was enough for him. Every decision I made, I made with the false certainty and courage of youth.

"Uno nunca sabe quien te va tocar," my Tía Lupe had said to me.

By the time Grandmother died, Lupe had full blown schizophrenia and was making up stories about people breaking into her room to harvest her eggs. She said she had a daughter who'd been born to another couple about three years ago. A year later, she committed suicide and I was left even more alone with her words.

My second marriage was even more violent. I remarried in 1999. He was a wrestling coach for high school students. He trained young men to use their bodies to conquer others.

Those moments when he let loose his skillset on me weren't nearly as scary as the other times when he overdosed on alcohol. I was 26 and as I used my key to enter the house, I felt the crunch of glass. I called for him. Called again. I looked in every room and found him in bed, foaming at the mouth.

There was another time when he was so drunk and upset, he caught my body from behind. He wrapped his arms around me, tightly. One arm wrapped around my waist. The other one, the one holding the chef's knife, wrapped around my neck.

"I love you. I love you. I love you," he said.

"I know," I sobbed.

"I love you. I love you."

"How about we get into bed? You look like you need rest."

Blood was puddling on the carpet, though I can't remember if it was his or mine. My skin doesn't remember and my mind refuses to recall.

"Okay," he said, "are you coming, too?"

"Yes. Yes."

"And you won't call the police?"

"No, of course not," I said. "We are going to sleep, right? We can think more clearly in the morning and talk."

"Okay," he said.

I walked him down the long hallway that led to our bedroom. There was a large vomit stain on the carpet where he had almost died some months ago. I settled him, then crawled into bed.

"I need to use the bathroom," I said, after I had pulled the covers up.

I crept out and into the bathroom. I remember that long walk down the hallway and how the floor was cold against the pads of my feet. I held myself tight and walked slowly, so he wouldn't suspect anything. I locked myself in. He had destroyed the house phone when he had thrown it against the wall. Now I looked for the phone I had hidden. The floor was splattered with blood. I called the police then.

I can tell other stories about that time, but what is most vivid in my mind isn't the bodily pain. It isn't the way he touched me when he was happy or angry. I don't remember any of that. What I remember is the slightness of my body as

I trembled down that hall. My body remembers that. Not only on that night, but on all those previous nights, when I tried not to sob as I realized I was terrified of the person I had to lie next to, and whom I called husband.

"Quien te va tocar?" Lupe wondered. Well, it wasn't about luck. It was about me and all the fucked up ways I had learned to hurt my body. The touch I had given myself had never been kind. And I expected the same from my husband. I re-enacted again and again what I had been taught. And no one I knew had kind relationships with their partners.

I got divorced again.

There is hope stored in the body, just like there is pain that hides within the creases of my wrinkles or folds of my body. It doesn't matter if I can remember or not. My body remembers.

On a road trip with my husband of 13 years, I take out my knitting.

"I don't know how to start this. I don't remember," I say.

"Maybe once you start?"

His hands remain at the steering wheel. But his voice caresses me. He is always stroking me with love. I take in his words. His words settle on my flesh. I stop thinking and feel instead.

My hands remember something but what the muscles know, the mind often doesn't. If there is something I have learned from abuse it's that the mind and body are not one. In times of crisis, they float away from one another like water droplets in the car windows. They come from the same rain, but they split, each taking their own path.

My skin remembers scraping and rhythm. As I start to move, my hands know what to do. Soon, I have started casting on. After that, my fingers know what to do. I breathe in and breathe out.

"My hands remembered," I tell my husband.

"Yeah, that can happen," he says.

"My brain didn't remember. My hands did."

He squeezes my hand gently. I'm in wonder for a bit. I revel in that wonder of touch that has been so meaningful in my life. While I wonder, my hands continue to knit. My logic kicks in and I think about all the times knitting has felt like a strand of beads getting counted through a mantra of hope. My fingers touch each strand and with each loop and release, my tension gives way. This kind of touch is as close to prayer as I ever get.

# Acknowledgements

I WISH TO EXPRESS MY sincere gratitude to Antioch University. In particular, I'd like to thank my mentors: Brad Kessler, Christine Hale, and Terry Wolverton. I also want to thank professors Gayle Brandeis, Ana Maria Spagna, and Sarah Van Arsdale, who always showed up for me and encouraged me not to be invisible.

I sincerely thank *The Nasiona* and lead publisher, Julián Esteban Torres López, who has been a nurturing and thoughtful partner in this process.

# About the Author

Mireya S. Vela is a Mexican-American creative non-fiction writer, storyteller, and artist in Los Angeles. *Vestiges of Courage* is her work of collected essays. In her work, Ms. Vela addresses the needs of immigrant Mexican families and the disparities they face every day. She tackles issues of inequity and how ingrained societal systems support the (ongoing) injustice that contributes to continuing poverty and abuse. Ms. Vela received her Bachelor's degree in English from Whitter College and received her Master of Fine Arts from Antioch University in 2018. In 2018, Ms. Vela's work was published in *Hippocampus Magazine* ("On the Bus"), *Noble / Gas Quarterly* ("Voiceless"), *Not Your Mother's Breastmilk* ("Legacy of Rape"), *The Nasiona* ("Doctores"), *Miracle Monocle* ("Touch : Tocar"), *Blanket Sea* ("Delusion"), *Cordella* ("Sick with Dog/God"), and *Collective Unrest* ("Tiger Says Meow" and "The Bridge"). In 2018, she received four Pushcart Prize nominations.

Ms. Vela is also a visual artist. Her work was featured in *The Nasiona* in 2018.

Twitter and Instagram: @mireyasvela

Visual Art website: mireyavela.com

# About *The Nasiona*

*Birds then came, bringing in **seeds**, and our pile became an oasis of life.*

*Pojawiły się ptaki, przynosząc **nasiona** i nasza skądinąd jałowa górka*

*stała się oazą życia. (Polish)*

*The Nasiona* is a community of creatives whose mission is to cultivate the seeds of nonfiction. We do this through a nonfiction literary magazine, podcast, and publishing house, as well as by offering editing services, literary contests, and an internship program.

In an age when telling the difference between reality and delusion is frighteningly labyrinthine, we focus on creative works based on facts, truth-seeking, human concerns, real events, and real people, with a personal touch.

From liminal lives to the marginalized, and everything in between, we glimpse into different, at times extraordinary, worlds to promote narrative-led nonfiction stories and art that explore the spectrum of human experience. We believe that the subjective can offer its own reality and reveal truths some facts can't discover.

We're a diversity-friendly organization that values multicultural and multi-experience perspectives on what it means to be human. We look to erase borders, tackle taboos, resist conventions, explore the known and unknown, and rename ourselves to claim ourselves.

We feature creative nonfiction and nonfiction poetry, book excerpts, a column on memoir writing, visual art, and interview interesting individuals from all over. We publish continuously, on a rolling basis, and accept submissions from emerging and established authors and content creators.

Our internship program aims to contribute to the development of editors, journalists, writers, scholars, and those interested in the publishing industry.

With our literary contests, we look to identify and celebrate some of the best original, unpublished creative nonfiction and nonfiction poetry out there.

We founded *The Nasiona* in the summer of 2018 in California. Though based in hilly San Francisco, the world is our home. Help us cultivate this pile of seeds and we'll do our best to create a worthy oasis for human life to not only exist but flourish.

*The Nasiona* depends on voluntary contributions from readers like you. We hope the value of our work to the community is worth your patronage. If you like what we do, please show this by financially supporting our work through our Patreon platform.

https://www.patreon.com/join/TheNasiona

Please follow *The Nasiona* on Twitter, Instagram, and Facebook for regular updates: @TheNasiona

https://thenasiona.com/

Made in the USA
Las Vegas, NV
04 December 2020

11982477R20154